**B5N2 from "Akagi" aircraft carrier, pilot: 2nd Lt Jinichi Goto**

Painted by: Marek Ryś

# Dariusz Paduch

# Nakajima B5N
# Kate

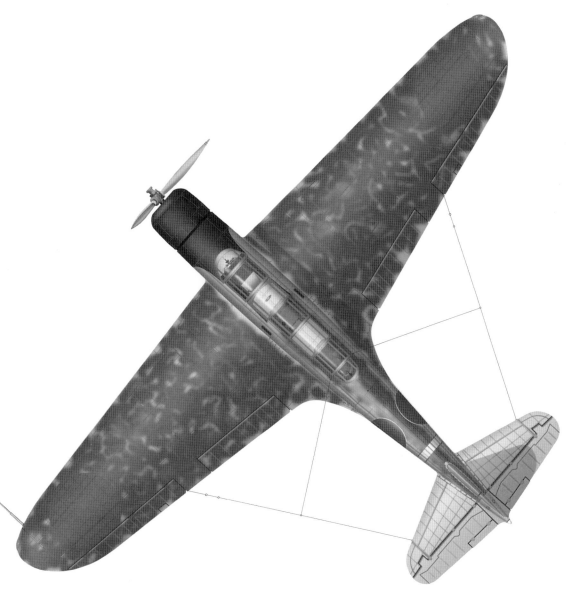

*To my Wife,*
*for Her understanding and support*

# MORE FROM KAGERO

**www.shop.kagero.pl**
• **phone + 4881 5012105**

Nakajima B5N Kate • Dariusz Paduch • First edition • LUBLIN 2021

Cover: **Marek Ryś** • Color profiles: **Alexey Valyaev-Zaitsev** • Drawings: **Anirudh Rao** • Photo: **Author's collection, Internet, Public domain, Kagero Archive** • Translation: **Stanisław Powała-Niedźwiecki** • DTP: **KAGERO STUDIO – Łukasz Maj**

**KAGERO Publishing**
Akacjowa 100, Turka, os. Borek, 20-258 Lublin 62, Poland, phone/fax: (+48) 81 501 21 05
www.kagero.pl • e-mail: kagero@kagero.pl, marketing@kagero.pl, shop@kagero.pl
w w w . k a g e r o . p l
Distribution: **KAGERO Publishing**

When Pacific War broke out, the Japanese naval aviation had the world's most modern torpedo bomber—the Nakajima B5N2. At that time, it was much better than the American Douglas TBD-1 *Devastator* and put the British Fairey *Swordfish* biplane one generation behind. The Japanese planes were faster, had better manoeuvrability, and could drop torpedoes from a greater height. After a successful debut at Pearl Harbour, B5Ns took part in all major naval battles up to 1944, permanently entering the history of aviation. Only at the turn of 1943/1944, this excellent plane began to be replaced by the modern Nakajima B6N *Tenzan*. But the road to B5N was not easy and was full of failures.

## Predecessors

The Japanese Imperial Navy very early saw the need to have a modern torpedo-bomber, but subsequent development programs did not meet the expectations of Kaigun Koku Hombu. In the early 1930s, the Imperial Navy aviation had huge problems with equipping units with the appropriate class of aircraft of this type. The first Mitsubishi torpedo-bomber, the 1MT1 triplane, turned out to be unsuccessful and inconvenient to use due to its size. Further constructions improved the situation only temporarily.

The deck torpedo-bombers constituted an important factor in the Japanese doctrine of sea aviation, therefore the efforts to develop a world-class torpedo-bomber were not ceased. However, the competitions for a new machine

announced every two years gave very poor results. In April 1932, Nakajima and Mitsubishi companies received the 7 Shi technical requirements for a new torpedo-bomber, but this time Kaigun Koku Hombu ordered the commencement of design work also at the Naval Aviation Arsenal in Yokosuka (Kaigun Kokusho) to protect against another failure. Soon there was a design for a fixed-undercarriage biplane with a mixed structure, powered by a Hiro Type 91 Model 2 V-engine with power of 750 hp. The assembly of the first prototype was completed the same year. Although it was a completely new design, the machine was given the designation "Modernized Type 13 Deck Torpedo-Bomber", implying that it was a development of the Mitsubishi B2M.

As feared, the results of the 7 Shi competition were tragic. Both Mitsubishi (3MT10) and Nakajima (B3N1) prototypes were lost in crashes, and Aichi's prototype—AB-8—which entered into the competition as a private venture, performed only slightly better than machines of that time. In this situation, despite the fact that the aircraft developed in Yokosuka proved difficult to fly during the tests and had great problems with maintaining air stability, it was decided to develop it further. In August 1933, the prototype was accepted for serial production. It was designated as "Type 92 Model 1 Deck Torpedo-Bomber" (B3Y1).

In total, about 130 aircraft of this type had been made by 1936, when production was halted. Type 92 Model 1 took an active part in the second Japanese Chinese conflict, taking off from the decks of aircraft carriers and land

B5N2 from Yokosuka Kokutai, 1943–1944. In 1944, these machines were replaced by newer Nakajima B6N *Tenzan*. [Author's collection]

Mitsubishi 1MT1 was an unsuccessful design and caused many problems in operation.
[Author's collection]

The Yokosuka B3Y1 torpedo-bomber entered mass production, although it was difficult to fly and had an unreliable engine.
[Author's collection]

bases. B3Y1 was plagued by frequent engine failures, and it quickly turned out that they were ineffective. It was clear that the successor should be seriously considered.

In 1934, the command of the Imperial Navy announced an urgent need for a new torpedo-bomber that could replace the "not-so-successful" B3Y1. In this situation, Kaigun Koku Hombu developed the specification 9 Shi. In February 1934, Mitsubishi and Nakajima were traditionally invited to participate in the competition. In

addition to them, the Yokosuka Naval Aviation Arsenal was also involved to develop its own project.

At Mitsubishi construction bureau, the development of the new aircraft was progressing fast. A team of designers led by Eng. Hajime Matsuhara, the creator of 3MT10, based on the earlier design, which accelerated the works enormously. The analysis of the causes of the 3MT10 failure showed that the aircraft had too much weight in relation to engine power. At the

Yokosuka B4Y1 planes took an active part in the second Japanese Chinese conflict. The photo shows the machine from 14th Kokutai during the flight over China. [Author's collection]

At the outbreak of the Pacific War, the Yokosuka B4Y1 torpedo bombers were used in training and second line units. [Author's collection]

same time flight tests showed that the radial engines are more reliable, and one of the main criticisms of earlier designs was the failure rate of the in-line engines. Taking these observations into account, Eng. Matsuhara decided to use a radial engine on the new Ka-12 torpedo-bomber (Ka-12 was a factory designation given to this machine), because, in addition to greater reliability, this solution allowed to reduce the weight of the aircraft. On the assumption that a proprietary product is better, the Mitsubishi A-9 engine, which still was developed, was chosen instead of a refined Nakajima Hikari 1 engine with similar power. The latter turned out to be a big failure. As early as August 1934, a prototype of the new aircraft was ready. It was a classic mixed-structure biplane with a fixed landing gear. The machine took off for the first time from the Kagamigahara airfield on August 25, 1934. After handing it over to the Navy for further trials, the aircraft was given the designation "9 Shi Experimental Torpedo-Bomber" (B4M1).

Shortly after the announcement of the 9 Shi's design objectives, Nakajima's engineers Takao Yoshoda and Yasuo Fukuda projected the new aircraft. It was given the factory designa-

tion "Q", and later the military designation "9 Shi Experimental Torpedo-Bomber" (B4N1). It was a classic fixed-undercarriage biplane with a mixed construction.

The work was delayed, and two prototypes were completed only in 1936. The first one was powered by the Nakajima Hikari 1 engine, and the second used the Nakajima Kotobuki 3 power unit. However, none of the above-mentioned planes met the assumed requirements and was not approved by the Imperial Navy.

The situation of the deck aviation, as in the case of the 7 Shi requirements, forced the mass production of the B4Y1 (developed in Kugisho). It was considered the best option, although it did not meet all the expectations.

At the Aviation Arsenal in Yokosuka, a team of designers working on the development of a new torpedo-bomber was headed by Eng. Sanae Kawasaki. The design of the machine, which was given the designation "9 Shi Experimental Torpedo-Bomber" (B4Y1), made it possible to install various types of engines. In order to make the construction pace as fast as possible, generally available materials and components were used during the construction. For this purpose, a new fuselage structure was developed,

## Basic tactical and technical data of Japanese torpedo-bomber aircraft

| | Mitsubishi 1MT1 | Aichi AB-8 | Yokosuka B3Y1 | Nkajima B3N1 | Yokosuka B4Y1 | Mitsubishi B4M1 | Nakajima B4N1 |
|---|---|---|---|---|---|---|---|
| Wingspan [m] | 13.26 | 14.0 | 13.51 | 13.5 | 15.00 | 14.8 | |
| Length [m] | 9.78 | 9.55 | 9.5 | 9.5 | 10.15 | 9.96 | |
| Height [m] | 4.46 | 3.67 | 3.73 | 3.8 | 4.36 | 3.94 | |
| Wing area [m²] | 43.0 | 48.3 | 50.0 | 50.0 | 50.0 | 54.0 | |
| **Mass [kg]** | | | | | | | |
| unladen | 1,370 | 1,770 | 1,850 | 2,000 | 2,000 | 2,000 | |
| take-off | 2,500 | 3,200 | 3,200 | 3,500 | 3,600 | 3,827 | |
| practical | 1,130 | 1,430 | 1,350 | 1,500 | 1,600 | 1,827 | |
| Surface load [kg/m²] | 58.14 | 66.25 | 64.0 | 76.0 | 72.0 | 70.87 | |
| Power load [kg/KM] | 5.56 | 5.33 | 4.27 | 4.28 | 4.29 | 5.28 | |
| Engine type | Napier *Lion* | Lorraine *Courlis* | Hiro Type 91 Model 2 | Nakajima *Kotobuki 3* | Hiro Type 91-I | Mitsubishi A-9 | Nakajima *Hikari 1* |
| Engine take-off power [KM] | 450 | 600 | 750 | 640 | 620 | 725 | 730 |
| **Speed [km/h]** | | | | | | | |
| maximum | 209 | 236 | 218 | 222 | 278 | 241 | |
| cruise | 130 | 170 | | | | | |
| Climb time [min, s] | 13'30"[1] | | | 12'00"[2] | 14'00"[2] | 14'33"[2] | |
| Practical ceiling [m] | 6,000 | | 6,000 | 5,500 | 6,000 | | |
| Range [km] | | | 1,570 | | 1,574 | | |
| Flight duration [h, min] | 2 h 20' | | 4 h 30' | 6 h | 8 h | 6 h 17' | |
| Crew | 1 | 3 | 3 | 3 | 3 | 3 | 3 |
| Armament | No gunnery armament; One 400 kg bomb or one torpedo | One fixed MG and one flexible MG Type 87 7.7 mm; Up to 800 kg of bombs or one torpedo | One fixed MG Type 89 7.7 and one flexible MG 7.7 mm; One 500 kg bomb or two 250 kg bombs, or six 30 kg bomb, or one torpedo | One fixed MG Type 89 7.7 mm; One 800 kg bomb or two 250 kg bombs, or one torpedo | One fixed MG Type 92 7.7 mm; Up to 800 kg of bombs or one torpedo | Two fixed MGs Type 89 7.7 mm and one flexible MG Type 89; Up to 800 kg of bombs or one torpedo | One fixed MG and one flexible MG Type 89 kal. 7.7 mm; One 500 kg bomb or two 250 kg bombs, or six 30 kg bombs, or one torpedo |

1 – at an altitude of 3,050 m
2 – at an altitude of 3,000 m

## Basic tactical and technical data of the Mitsubishi B1M

| | B1M1 | B1M2 | B1M3 |
|---|---|---|---|
| Wingspan [m] | 14.77 | 14.77 | 14.78 |
| Length [m] | 9.77 | 10.06 | 10.12 |
| Height [m] | 3.5 | 3.52 | 3.52 |
| Wing area [m²] | 59.0 | 57.0 | 57.0 |
| **Mass [kg]** | | | |
| unladen | 1,442 | 1,765 | 1,750 |
| take-off | 2,697 | 2,850 | 2,900 |
| operational | 1,255 | 1,085 | 1,150 |
| Surface load [kg/m²] | 45,71 | 50,0 | 50,88 |
| Power load [kg/KM] | 5,99 | 4,75 | 4,83 |
| Engine type | Napier *Lion* | Mitsubishi/Hispano-Suiza Type Hi | Mitsubishi/Hispano-Suiza Type Hi |
| Take-off power [KM] | 450 | 600 | 600 |
| **Speed [km/h]** | | | |
| max. at an altitude of 1,000 m | 210 | 194 | 196 |
| cruise at an altitude of 1,000 m | 175 | 162 | 164 |
| landing | | 138 | |
| Climb time to a 3,000 m [min, s] | | 20'00" | 17'00" |
| Practical range [m] | | 4,500 | |
| Maximum range [m] | | 3,100 | |
| Time duration [h, min] | 2 h 36' | 5 h | |
| Armament | Two flexible Vickers MGs 7,7 mm; Two 250 kg bombs or one torpedo | Two fixed and two flexible Vickers MGs 7,7 mm; Two 250 kg bombs or one torpedo | Two fixed and two flexible Vickers MGs 7,7 mm; Two 250 kg bombs or one torpedo |

and its tail and wings were adapted from the Kawanishi E7K1 reconnaissance seaplane. The plane had a mixed structure and a fixed landing gear. The pilot's cabin was uncovered, and the remaining cabins were covered with a common, richly glazed canopy. The first prototype, which was completed and flown in 1935, was powered by a 620 hp Hiro Type 91-I V-engine. Four more prototypes were built over the course of the following year. They had an increased wingspan and new power units. The second and third prototypes were powered by Nakajima Kotobuki 3 engine with a take-off power of 640 hp. Fourth and fifth prototype received Nakajima Hikari 2

| Basic tactical and technical data of the Mitsubishi B2M | | | |
|---|---|---|---|
| | 3MR4 | B2M1 | B2M2 |
| Wingspan [m] | 15.0 | 15.22 | 14.98 |
| Lenght [m] | 10.13 | 10.27 | 10.18 |
| Height [m] | 3.78 | 3.71 | 3.6 |
| Wing area [m²] | 55.0 | 55.00 | 49.00 |
| Mass [kg] | | | |
| unladen | 1,927 | 2,260 | 2,180 |
| take-off | 3,402 | 3,600 | 3,600 |
| practical | 1,475 | 1,340 | 1,420 |
| Surface load [kg/m²] | 61.85 | 65.45 | 73.5 |
| Power load [KM] | 5.67 | 6.0 | 6.0 |
| Engine type | Mitsubishi/Hispano-Suiza Type Hi | Mitsubishi/Hispano-Suiza Type Hi | Mitsubishi/Hispano-Suiza Type Hi |
| Take-off power [KM] | 650 | 650 | 650 |
| Speed [km/h] | | | |
| maximum | 216 | 212[1] | 228[1] |
| cruise | | 182[1] | 185[1] |
| landing | 96 | | |
| Climb time to a 3,000 m [min, s] | | 18'00" | 12'00" |
| Practical ceiling [m] | 4,260 | | |
| Range [km] | | | |
| normal | | 1,020 | 1,060 |
| maximum | 1,286 | 1,780 | 1,760 |
| Crew | 3 | 3 | 3 |
| Armament | One fixed MG and one flexible MG Vickers 7.7 mm; Up to 800 kg of bombs or one torpedo | One fixed MG and one flexible MG Vickers 7.7 mm; Up to 800 kg of bombs or one torpedo | One fixed MG and one flexible MG Vickers 7.7 mm; Up to 800 kg of bombs or one torpedo |

1 – at an altitude of 1,000 m

radial engine with a take-off power of 840 hp. The tests showed that the last two prototypes had the best performance, and they were just selected for the comparative tests with the B4M1 and B4N1. In November 1936, Kaigun Koku Hombu officially accepted the B4Y1 prototype into series production, giving it the designation "Type 96 Torpedo-Bomber". As with the B3Y1, the production of the new machine was split between Nakajima, Mitsubishi, and the Hiro Naval Aviation Arsenal (Kaigun Kokusho). Production was discontinued in 1938. A total of 205 copies were built.

Until 1940, the B4Y1 aircraft operated from the "Akagi", "Kaga", "Sōryū" and "Ryūjō" carriers, actively participating in the second Japanese Chinese conflict. They were not very modern and significantly differed in performance from the Mitsubishi A5M deck fighters. That is why the cooperation of the individual airborne units was very difficult. After the outbreak of the Pacific War, the B4Y1 planes were already moved to second line and training units. Only the oldest Japanese carrier, "Hōshō", still had eight machines of this type, but after commencing combat operations, it was rearmed with Nakajima B5N2 torpedo-bombers. In the Allied code, B4Y1 received the designation *Jean*.

# Birth of B5N

In 1936, the obsolete and "emergency" torpedo-bombers were replaced with newer B4Y1s, but this was a temporary solution. The new plane had a top speed of 277 km/h and a range of 1,574 km, which was enough at that time, but it could not be enough in future. In 1935, the monoplane fighter, later known as the Mitsubishi A5M *Claude*, made its first flights, reaching a speed of 449 km/h at an altitude of 3,000 m and proving that the era of biplanes came to an end.

In 1935, Kaigun Koku Hombu released the technical order of the 10 Shi containing radically new requirements resulting from a completely new approach to the subject of a deck torpedo-bomber. The given characteristics were much higher than any aircraft of this type developed so far. The set task was very ambitious, but both Mitsubishi and Nakajima decided to try their hand at this competition.

The 10 Shi requirements expected that the new airplane should reach a maximum speed of not less than 330 km/h and have an overall performance impossible to achieve by a biplane. During the tests of the A5M *Claude* there were problems with deviations from the course in the last stages of the landing approach, which could be very dangerous for the aircraft landing on the carrier, but it was found that the problem could be solved by the use of flaps, which at that time were considered as novelty, although in their early form they were already used during the World War I.

A great help for the constructors was getting acquainted with the Northrop Gamma 5A plane. Its only prototype (registration number X 14997) was purchased in order to learn about new technologies. On October 29, 1935, it was sent from USA to Japan. The machine was handed over to the Navy, where it was given the des-

Northrop Gamma 5A. The only prototype of this machine was bought by the Japanese to learn about new technical solutions and technologies. [Author's collection]

First prototype of Nakajima B5N1 in flight. Note the asymmetrical suspension of the torpedo. [Author's collection]

ignation BXN1. During the tests, the plane was crashed and completely destroyed, but before it happened, a lot of valuable information was collected.

The Gamma 5A, for its times, had many innovative solutions. It used, among other novelties, the results of the flap work carried out at NACA in 1933. In the USA, its design was modernized by adding a retractable landing gear and a more powerful engine, thus creating the Northrop A-17 light bomber, some of which were used by the RAF during World War II under the designation *Nomad*. The Gamma 5A design solutions have also been used as a starting point by Douglas in their TBD *Devastator* and SBD *Dauntless* projects. Eng. Jiro Horikoshi (the creator of the famous A6M *Zero*) believed that this plane was the most important for the Japanese from all those bought abroad in the 1930s. The influence of the data gathered during the analysis of its construction and capabilities was enormous on further Japanese designs.

The 10 Shi specification stated that the wingspan of the new aircraft should not exceed 16 m, and 7.5 m when folded to be hangared. These limitations were due to the size of the lift platforms on Japanese carriers. The plane should be capable of carrying 800 kg of bombs or torpedoes, and the defence armament was to consist of one 7.7 mm machine gun. At an altitude of 2,000 m, the maximum speed was to be 330 km/h. Normal flight duration should

be 4 hours, while on economic speed of 250 km/h, the maximum flight duration should last 7 hours. The new machine was to be powered by a Nakajima Hikari or Mitsubishi Kinsei radial engine, and the crew was to be three people.

Earlier failures in the development of a modern torpedo-bomber under the 7 and 9 Shi programs made the 10 Shi program practically the last chance to catch up with the world leaders in this field and Kaigun Koku Hombu had high hopes for it. The Naval Aviation Command was well aware that in the event of a war with any enemy except China, there would be a catastrophe, as the biplanes are not only outdated, but also unable to fulfil their tasks. A critical situation arose. Time was running and the Japanese lagged further and further behind their likely opponent.

Two companies took part in the competition: Nakajima Hikoki Kabushiki Kaisha and Mitsubishi Jukogyo Kabushiki Kaisha. Shortly after the competition was announced, the Nakajima team of designers presented a preliminary design of the machine, which was given the factory designation Type K. The aircraft was to be an all-metal, cantilever low-wing, with a working sheathing and a hydraulically retractable main landing gear. The landing gear mechanism of the future B5N was based on the solutions used in the Northrop A-17, and the B5N itself was one of the first aircraft of this type in Japan. The long, covered cabin housed three crew members: a pilot, a bombardier-navigator, and a radioman-machine gunner. The wing with a trapezoidal outline was divided into a centre wing and two hydraulically folding consoles. When folded, they overlap over the richly glazed canopy. Thanks to this solution, the plane needed much less space in the carrier's hangar. Such a complicated hydraulic system was used in Japan for the first time, therefore the problems related to its functioning that arose during the tests were not surprising and were successfully solved, while the experience gained was used in later designs.

In the first draft of the preliminary design, the fuselage of the plane was slim, but long, so the plane would barely fit on the lift platform. Therefore, in the second draft of the project, the fuselage was shortened to 10.3 m and Fowler flaps and a three-bladed metal constant speed propeller with variable pitch were used. The plane was to be powered by a Nakajima Hikari 2 9-cylinder radial engine with a take-off power of 840 hp, equipped with a NACA cowling, characterized by a low aerodynamic drag.

The design of the new aircraft in this form was submitted to the competition. Soon it was approved, and the construction of the prototype began. The assembly was completed in December 1936. It was given the military designation "10 Shi Experimental Torpedo-Bomber" (B5N1). The machine first took off in January 1937. Despite the use of a relatively low-power engine, the aircraft developed a high, at that time, top speed of 370 km/h, far exceeding the specifications. The designers from Nakamura's team, however, were far from euphoric, because during the tests, both on the ground and in the air, many defects were revealed. The hydraulic system for folding the main landing gear and wingtips was the most problematic issue, but there were many more minor problems, some of which were very difficult to fix. One of the reasons was the fact of using many new solutions in the construction of the aircraft, which were not fully refined and, as a result, caused problems. However, very good performance and flight properties spoke in favour of the project.

The Naval Aviation Command was very incredulous about Nakajima's innovative approach, fearing that the complex structure would make the aircraft more difficult to operate and increase its failure rate. Problems with the hydraulic system seemed to confirm these concerns. Considering the above, the designers were instructed to simplify the construction of the second prototype. Instead of a hydraulic one, a somewhat crude but reliable manual wing folding mechanism was used, and Fowler flaps, which also caused problems, were replaced by classic slotted flaps. Integral fuel tanks with a capacity of 1,150 l were placed in the centre wing, and the engine was switched to a Hikari 3 with a take-off power of 720 hp. It was not planned to use any protection for the cockpit and fuel tanks. In order to enable the aircraft to carry bombs or torpedoes (depending on the need), various suspension nodes were developed, which the technical staff could quickly replace or remove.

The good forward visibility from the cockpit was essential for the deck plane pilot. Unfortunately, with the tail down, it was very poor on B5N1, that's why during take-off and landing the pilot's seat could be raised so his head was levelled with the upper edge of the windscreen. The navigator-bombardier/observer sat

Nakajima B5N1 with folded wings and torpedo under the fuselage. [Author's collection]

After folding, the B5N wingtips overlapped each other over the richly glazed canopy of the crew compartment. [Author's collection]

behind the pilot, facing forward, and had two small windows in the sides of his cabin to allow observation of fuel consumption indicators located on the upper surface of the centre wing. In order to target the bomb drop, he opened a small door in the floor. The radioman-machine gunner sat with his back to the direction of flight, most often with a retracted machine gun

Details of the B5N1 wing folding mechanism. [Author's collection]

and a closed cockpit cover, which improved the aerodynamics of the aircraft. Early radio stations operated at low frequencies and were equipped with a long, droppable antenna. Communication between crew members was via a voice tube, and oxygen equipment was usually not fitted.

In this form, the second prototype began comparative tests with its rival—the Mitsubishi B5M1, and then went into the mass production.

The second B5N1 prototype had hand-folded wings. In this form, the machine was sent for comparative tests with the competing Mitsubishi B5M1. [Author's collection]

B5N1 Model 11 from the "Sōryū" aircraft carrier during combat trials in northern China, year 1938. [Author's collection]

## Competitor

In accordance with the design requirements of the 10 Shi specification, Mitsubishi has developed an aircraft design, which has been given the plant designation Ka-16, and the military "10 Shi Experimental Torpedo-Bomber" (B5M1). The machine had a more traditional design, which made it easier to build and operate. The plane had a fixed landing gear covered with fair-

Nakajima B5N1 Model 11 of 14th Kokutai during operation in China (1938–1939). The plane has a two-colour camouflage on the upper surfaces. [Author's collection]

Nakajima B5N1 taking off from „Akagi" carrier. [Author's collection]

The competing Mitsubishi B5M1 had a more traditional fixed undercarriage design. [Author's collection]

ings similar to those used on the Aichi D3A dive bomber. The elliptical wings were fitted with crocodile flaps and from the beginning were folded by hand in the middle of the span. The crew, as in the case of the Nakajima B5N1, consisted of three people. The Ka-16 prototype was powered by the Mitsubishi Kinsei 3 engine with a take-off power of 840 hp. Fuel tanks capacity was 1,000 l.

Both machines performed well during the tests. The B5N1 developed faster, but the B5M1 seemed more reliable. It was impossible to unequivocally indicate the winner of the competition, because each plane was both inferior and superior to the competitor in something. Initially, the Mitsubishi B5M1, as more conventional and easier to use, received greater recognition from the command of the Imperial Navy. Comparative tests were slightly better for the B5N1, but problems with the hydraulic system caused concerns about the operational properties of such a complex structure. The problems were eliminated at Nakajima by resigning from hydraulic folding system of the wings in favour of manual one, but the Kaigun Koku Hombu still had doubts about the suitability and value of the B5N1.

To minimize the risk of failure in this extremely important development program for the Imperial Navy, it was decided to put both aircraft into mass production. Mitsubishi Ka-16 received the military designation "Type 97-2 Deck Torpedo-Bomber" (B5M1 Model 2). The plane could carry up to 800 kg of bombs or a torpedo, and it was armed with a single 7.7 mm Type 92 machine gun.

The winner of the competition was to be selected on the basis of the results of the operation of aircraft in line units. The second Japanese Chinese conflict was just underway, so both machines were sent to China. The trials were conducted on aircraft carriers and in land-based units, where the planes were used to support ground forces. Although it was not its primary role, the B5N1 proved itself well as a tactical bomber, and the pilots claimed that it stays firmly in the air, obeys the stick well, and thanks to a special sight in the cabin floor, it is possible to bomb accurately and determine whether the target was hit or not.

Defensive armament, consisting of one Type 92 machine gun, was fully sufficient in terms of fighting conditions in China. The Japanese had absolute air superiority, though. The disadvantage was the lack of offensive, firing forward weapons, which made it impossible to shoot at enemy positions. The previously noticed shortcomings related to the lack of protection of the crew cockpit, engine and fuel tanks also made themselves known, but no Japanese aircraft at that time could boast of armour or patronized fuel tanks.

Fighting in China identified the aircraft's capabilities and dispelled doubts about its reliability, as it turned out that the failure rate of the B5N1 was relatively low. The choice of the winner of the competition was most likely due to the greater modernization potential of the Nakajima B5N1, also the new version of this machine has already been prepared—the B5N2—which should have better performance thanks to the more powerful engine. It was also not without significance that the Mitsubishi construction team was at that time overloaded with work related to the modernization of the A5M deck fighter and designing a new dive bomber according to the 11 Shi specification, which Aichi ultimately won with its D3A. The plant

The B5M1 from the beginning had hand-folded wings. The photo shows a machine from Suzuka Kokutai, 1938. [Author's collection]

The Imperial Navy Command initially thought that the simpler design of the B5M1 would make it more reliable. [Author's collection]

also started a preliminary work on the fighter program 12 Shi.

Mitsubishi B5M1 production was carried out in 1937 at the Oemashi plant (65 units) and the 11th Naval Arsenal (according to various sources, 50 to 80 units were produced here). The machines produced at the Mitsubishi plant in Oemashi, instead of the Kinsei 3 engine, received the MK8D Kinsei 43 with a take-off power of 1,000 hp and fuel tanks with a capacity of 1,200 l. Ironically, the B5M1 produced in series had similar or better performance than the competing B5N1, however, the decision to discontinue production of the B5M1 has not changed. The competition for the new deck torpedo-bomber was over, and the winner was the Nakajima B5N, which became the standard armament of Japanese aircraft carriers and went into mass production. A little later, the Americans gave it the code designation *Kate*.

During the Pacific War, B5M1s briefly operated from land bases in Southeast Asia, patrolling for enemy submarines, and were later withdrawn to training and support units. In 1942, they were given the new designation—B5M1 Model 61. Initially, the Allies considered this aircraft as a version of the Nakajima B5N, therefore they gave it the same code designation. When it was realized that it was a completely different design, the code was changed to *Mabel*, but later reverted to the old designation *Kate 61*.

## Serial production and further development

The B5N1 aircraft of the first production series did not differ from the second prototype. They were given the military designation "Type 97-1 Deck Torpedo-Bomber" (B5N1 Mod-

Mitsubishi B5M1 of Suzuka Kokutai. [Author's collection]

At the beginning of the war, the B5M1 *Mabel* was used in combat during anti-submarine patrols. [Author's collection]

el 1), which, after changing the designation system, was changed to B5N1 Model 11. Machines of the second and third production series were also practically the same as the second prototype. Only the ineffective trailing antenna of the radio station was replaced with an antenna stretched between the mast on the canopy and the vertical stabilizer.

The new plane quickly became available to aircraft carriers of the Imperial Navy and land-based units. B5N1 was sent to China for baptism of fire. Instead of fighting warships, they supported ground troops. The conclusions from the experience gained at that time confirmed the high value of the aircraft, but the weak opponent's resistance (the Japanese dominated the air, and the anti-aircraft defence of the Chinese troops was symbolic) did not reveal the basic flaws of the aircraft, such as high sensitivity to enemy fire due to the lack of armour and protected fuel tanks, and too weak defensive armament. If the Nakajima B5N1 aircraft were to operate in Europe, their losses would certainly be much greater. The subsequent course of the fighting over the Pacific painfully revealed all these shortcomings, but the reinforcement of the armament and armour of the machine would have a negative impact on its performance. The most important conclusion drawn from the course of the fighting in China was to dispel Kaigun Koku Hombu's doubts about the reliability of the aircraft and to decide to discontinue production of the competing Mitsubishi B5M1.

The experience gained in China was also used in the development of a new version of

The combat service of the B5M1 was short. Aircraft was soon transferred to secondary tasks. [Author's collection]

the aircraft, which was given the designation "Deck Torpedo-Bomber Type 97-3 Model 12" (B5N2 Model 12). Work began in early 1939. The construction of the prototype was completed in November, and the prototype was flown in December. Externally, the new plane differed from its predecessor with a clearly changed silhouette in the nose part of the fuselage. This was caused by the use of a new 14-cylinder Nakajima NK1A Sakae 11 (Ha-35-11) engine with a take-off power of 940 hp. This engine not only developed more power, but also had a smaller diameter than the previously used Hikari, which forced the use of a new cowling. Side benefits of using the new engine were improved forward visibility from the cockpit and reduced frontal drag. The propeller hub was covered with a small cap, which was usually dismantled in units. The remaining elements of the airframe remained unchanged.

To the great disappointment of the designers, the use of a new engine with much more power only slightly improved the aircraft's performance. Nevertheless, the B5N2 was accepted and went into series production in early 1940. The main argument for such a decision was the exceptional reliability of the new engine, which was especially important for long cruises over the sea.

Shortly before the outbreak of the Pacific War, the B5N2 was used by most Japanese aircraft carriers, replacing the old Yokosuka B4Y1 and the earlier Nakajima B5N1 version. During the first months of combat, the B5N2 aircraft achieved many successes, but also suffered heavy losses. By April 1942, 200 machines of this type were lost, half of which were operational losses. Further combat operations, such as the Battle of Midway, or prolonged fighting in the Solomon Islands region, brought more losses. In 1944, the B5N2 was replaced by the new Nakajima B6N torpedo-bomber, but due to the high landing speed of the B6N, there were

The new Nakajima B5N1 torpedo-bomber planes quickly found their way into the aircraft carriers and ground units. In the photo B5N1 Model 11 from Yokosuka Hikotai, 1939 [Author's collection]

## Basic tactical and technical data of Nakajima B5N and Mitsubishi B5M

| | Nakajima B5N1 I prototype | Nakajima B5N1 Model 11 | Nakajima B5N1-K | Nakajima B5N2 Model 12 | Mitsubishi Ka-14 (prototype) | Mitsubishi B5M1 |
|---|---|---|---|---|---|---|
| Wingspan [m] | 15.52 | 15.52 | 15.52 | 15.52 | 16.00 | 15.3 |
| Length [m] | 10.3 | 10.3 | 10.3 | 10.3 | 10.3 | 10.23 |
| Height [m] | 3.7 | 3.7 | 3.7 | 3.6 | 3.7 | 3.72 |
| Wing area [m²] | 37.69 | 37.69 | 37.69 | 37.69 | 40.3 | 39.64 |
| Mass [kg] unladen | 2,106 | 2,099 | 2,153 | 2,279 | 2,200 | 2,342 |
| take-off normal | 3,650 | 3,700 | 3,700 | 3,800 | 3,820 | 4,000 |
| max. for take-off practical (max.) | 1,544 | 4,015 | 1,547 | 4,130 | 1,620 | 4,400 |
| | | 1,601 | | 1,521 | | 1,658 |
| Surface load [kg/m²] | 96.84 | 98.17 | 98.17 | 100.82 | 94.78 | 105.4 |
| Power lowad [kg/KM] | 5.21 | 4.8 | 4.8 | 3.8 | 5.31 | 4.0 |
| Engine type | Nakajima *Hikari 2* | Nakajima *Hikari 3* | Nakajima *Hikari 3* | Nakajima *Sakae 11* | Mitsubishi *Kinsei 3* | Mitsubishi *Kinsei 43* |
| Take-off power [KM] | 840 | 720 | 720 | 940 | 840 | 1000 |
| Speed [km/h] maximum | 370[1] | 350[3] | 346[4] | 378[4] | 353[5] | 381[6] |
| cruise | 256[2] | 256[2] | 259[2] | 259[1] | 228[2] | 256[2] |
| landing | 111 | 111 | 115 | 113 | 115 | 118 |
| Climb time to a 3,000 m [min, s] | 7'50" | 7'50" | 7'55" | 7'40" | 8'17" | 7'05" |
| Practical ceiling [m] | 7,400 | 7,400 | 7,660 | 8,260 | 6,250 | 8,260 |
| Range [km] normal | 1,095 | 1,220 | 1,160 | 1,280 | 1,076 | 1,200 |
| maximum | 2,260 | 2,150 | 2,100 | 2,280 | 1,220 | 2,320 |
| Flight duration [h, min] | 4 h 20' | 4 h 20' | 8 h 40' | 6 h 30' | 8 h 48' | 9 h 13' |
| Crew | 3 | 3 | 3 | 3 | 3 | 3 |
| Armament | One flexible MG Type 92 7.7 mm; Up to 800 kg of bombs or one torpedo Type 91 | One flexible MG Type 92 7.7 mm; Up to 800 kg of bombs or one torpedo Type 91 | One flexible MG Type 92 7.7 mm; Up to 800 kg of bombs or one torpedo Type 91 | One flexible MG Type 92 7.7 mm; Up to 800 kg of bombs or one torpedo Type 91 | One flexible MG Type 92 7.7 mm; Up to 800 kg of bombs or one torpedo Type 91 | One flexible MG Type 92 7.7 mm; Up to 800 kg of bombs or one torpedo Type 91 |

1 – at an altitude of 3,000 m
2 – at an altitude of 2,000 m
3 – at an altitude of 2,380 m
4 – at an altitude of 3,600 m
5 – at an altitude of 1,510 m
6 – at an altitude of 2,200 m

**The experience gained during the operations of the B5N1 in China did not reveal its main disadvantages, however, they were used in the design of the new version of this machine. [Author's collection]**

New engine changed the silhouette of the B5N2. [Kagero Archive]

Trainer B5N1-K from Kasumigaura Kokutai. 1941 [Author's collection]

still B5N2s on board of the small aircraft carriers. Along with other machines, they actively participated in one of the last aircraft carrier battles in the Philippine Sea.

The Nakajima B5N aircraft was characterized by high reliability and longevity, therefore, when the B5N1 units began to be withdrawn from the late 1942—early 1943, it was decided to use these machines to anti-submarines patrols in areas beyond the range of Allied aviation. In 1944, the B5N1 was transferred to the training units, and in the patrol units their place was taken over by the B5N2. Some of them were equipped with a primitive K4 radar and a Jikitanchiki magnetic anomaly detector. The radar antennas were placed on the sides of the rear fuselage and on the leading edges of the wings. The additional equipment theoretically increased the effectiveness of operations, especially in difficult weather conditions, but in practice, the effectiveness of the magnetic anomaly detector was low, if the plane did not fly 9–12 m above the sea surface.

The withdrawn B5N1 was widely used in aviation schools, where young naval aviators improved their skills at the final stage of training. On the basis of the B5N1, a special training version was developed—B5N1-K—and the necessary modifications were made by Nakajima plants. B5N planes were also used for towing targets, and during the research of the special Yokosuka Chikara training glider. At the end of the war, the B5N was used again to fight enemy ships. Some of the surviving machines were used for the Kamikaze attacks.

Between 1936 and 1941, Nakajima produced 669 B5N1s, B5N1-Ks and B5N2s. In 1942, the Aichi Takei Denki K.K. plant in Nagoya and Dai-Juichi Kaigun Kokusho began producing those planes under the license (respectively 200 and 280 B5N2s built) and continued it until 1943. A total of 1,149 B5N aircraft (including 30 B5N1-K) were built.

## Brief technical description

The single-engine Nakajima B5N deck torpedo-bomber was an all-metal, cantilever low-wing, with a retractable single-leg main landing

Some of the withdrawn from service B5N1s were converted into the training B5N1-K. The photo shows a machine from Kasumigaura Kokutai. 1941 [Author's collection]

Nakajima B5N1 of Kure Kokutai during the Battle of the Santa Cruz Islands. October 26, 1942 [Author's collection]

Certain number of the B5N2s used for anti-submarine patrols were equipped with radar and a magnetic anomaly detector. The photo shows the radar antennas on the leading edge of the wings. [Author's collection]

gear. The sheathing of the plane was metal, except for the ailerons and rudders, which were covered with cloth. The trapezoidal foldable wing was equipped with slotted flaps and was divided into a centre wing and two consoles. The cockpit of the three-person crew was covered with a common, richly glazed canopy. The plane had no armour, and the fuel tanks were not patronized. The aircraft was equipped with a standard set of navigational and control instruments, and a Type 96 Mk. 3 radio (later Type 2 Mk. 3). Some anti-submarine machines were equipped with a K4 radar and a Jikitanchiki magnetic anomaly detector.

**B5N2 Model 12 equipped with radar, captured and tested by the Allies. A radar antenna is visible on the side of the fuselage. [Author's collection]**

**The Nakajima B5N fuselage construction with visible frames and longerons. [Author's collection]**

Drive unit:

B5N1—first prototype, one Nakajima Hikari 2 9-cylinder radial engine with a take-off power of 840 hp and 800 hp at an altitude of 3,500 m, metal, three-blade, metal propeller with variable pitch and a diameter of 3.3 m, fuel tank capacity—1,150 l.

B5N1—second prototype, B5N1 Model 11, B5N1-K, one 9-cylinder Nakajima Hikari 3 radial engine with a take-off power of 720 hp and 840 hp at an altitude of 3,000 m, three-blade metal propeller with variable pitch and a diameter of 3.3 m, fuel tank capacity—1,150 l (B5N1-K—700 l).

B5N2 Model 12—one 14-cylinder Nakajima NK1A Sakae 11 radial engine (Ha-35-11) with 940 hp take-off power and 970 hp at 3,000 m altitude, 3-blade metal variable-pitch propeller, 3.2 m diameter, fuel tank capacity—1,160 m.

Both the Hikari and Sakae engines had exhaust manifolds, however, the late production B5N2 featured Sakae 11 engines with individual exhaust pipes.

The aircraft was armed with a single 7.7 mm Type 92 flexible machine gun, mounted in the cockpit of the radioman-machine gunner. On the external suspension nodes, the plane could carry one Type 91 457 mm torpedo, weighing 800 kg, or various combinations of standard Japanese bombs weighing up to 800 kg (one bomb weighing up to 800 kg, e.g., the Type 99 armour-piercing bomb, or two 250 kg bombs, e.g., a Type 88 land bomb, or six 60 kg bombs, e.g., Type 2). The racks replacement or torpedo conversion to bombs, or vice versa, was not easy and could take more than two hours. Type 90 Mk. 1 sight was installed in the floor of the navigator-bombardier cabin.

## On the way to Pearl Harbor

The combat debut of the Nakajima B5N torpedo-bomber took place in late 1938, when these machines were used as tactical bombers

The cockpit of the B5N was covered by a richly glazed canopy. [Author's collection]

The pilot's cabin of the B5N2 was equipped with a standard set of controls and navigational instruments. [Author's collection]

The instrument panel in the cockpit of the Nakajima B5N2. Sight is dismounted. [Author's collection]

Port side of the Nakajima B5N2 pilot's cockpit. [Author's collection]

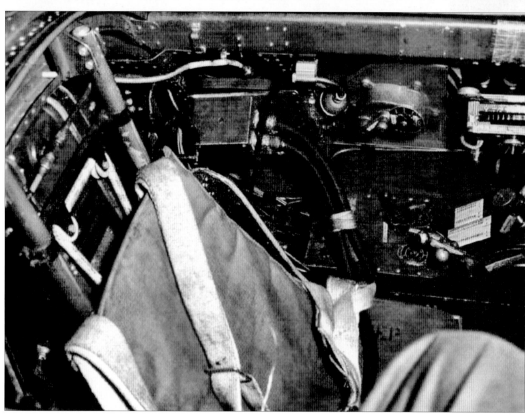

The interior of the B5N2 pilot's cockpit. [Author's collection]

in the Hankou area of China. In fall of 1940, with the consent of the Vichy authorities, Japanese troops were transferred to French Indochina and a small number of B5N2s operated from local airfields to bomb Chiang Kai-shek troops in southern China, but these activities did not allow the aircraft to be used in their essential role, and the time for real trial and large-scale action was yet to come.

The Japanese attack on the American base at Pearl Harbor was the first part of a grand plan to attack the enemy in various areas of the Pacific. The main goal was to seize oil and other resources that would allow Japan to carry out long-term hostilities. The attack was synchronized with the blows south towards the Philippines, Hong Kong, Singapore and the Dutch West Indies.

In 1932, Admiral Schofield conducted 14 tactical exercises of the Pacific Fleet in Hawaiian waters. Aircraft from US carriers unexpectedly attacked the base at Pearl Harbor, completely surprising the forces on the island. The success of the American admiral was noticed by Admiral Isoroku Yamamoto, who was able to draw the right conclusions from it, paying attention to

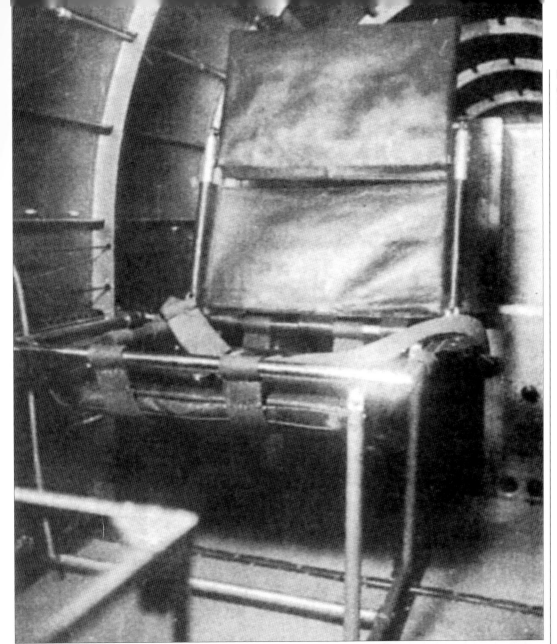

Navigator-bombardier's seat
of Nakajima B5N2.
[Author's collection]

Type 90 Mk. 1 sight mounted
in the floor of the navigator's
cockpit of the B5N2.
[Author's collection]

The K4 radar block in the navigator's cockpit of the B5N2. [Author's collection]

Left leg and wheel of Nakajima's B5N main landing gear. [Author's collection]

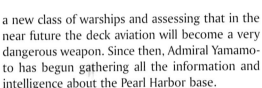

The way of mounting the undercarriage and tail wheel absorber of the Nakajima B5N. [Author's collection]

Nakajima Hikari Engine 3. [Public Domain]

a new class of warships and assessing that in the near future the deck aviation will become a very dangerous weapon. Since then, Admiral Yamamoto has begun gathering all the information and intelligence about the Pearl Harbor base.

Pacific Fleet Commander Admiral Richardson thought it was risky to base a fleet in Hawaii, but his safety concerns and lengthy clearing up efforts were ignored and eventually he was dismissed from office. On February 1, 1941, he was replaced by Admiral Husband E. Kimmel, who perfectly understood the lesson given to his predecessor and did not speak aloud about the need to recall the Pacific Fleet from Hawaii.

At the same time, in Japan, Admiral Yamamoto, in complete secrecy, began thinking about a plan to attack Hawaii. Unlike the traditional school represented by the majority of staff members, he was a supporter of modern warfare in which aircraft carriers would play a major role.

On the night of November 11–12, 1940, 21 obsolete British Fairey *Swordfish* aircraft attacked most of the Italian warships anchored in the Gulf of Taranto. The attack was carried out in two waves (1st wave—12 aircraft, 2nd wave—9 aircraft, one of which had to turn back shortly after take-off due to engine failure) and lasted about an hour. As a result of the damage, three battleships were taken out of service for several months, changing the balance of power in the Mediterranean Sea for a short time. The British lost only two planes during the attack.

The incident made a great impression on the Secretary of the US Navy, F. Knox, who be-

Type 91 torpedo 457 mm suspended under the fuselage of the B5N1 Model 11. [Author's collection]

The Nakajima B5N could carry bombs weighing up to 800 kg instead of a torpedo. The photo shows six 60 kg bombs hung on the racks. [Author's collection]

Sixty-kilogram Type 97 bomb
under the fuselage of a B5N.
[Author's collection]

US Navy Pearl Harbor base
and Hickam Field, Hawaii.
October 13, 1941. Among
the ships visible are five
battleships and the aircraft
carrier USS "Enterprise"
(CV-6). [Author's collection]

Admiral Isoroku Yamamoto very early considered the advantages of using a new kind of warships—aircraft carriers. The photo shows the admiral on board the battleship "Nagato", 1941. [Author's collection]

lieved that in the event of a war with Japan, similar events could take place at Pearl Harbor. Nobody in the US took Knox's arguments seriously. Paradoxically, his comments were appreciated by Admiral Yamamoto who learned lessons that would cost Americans dearly. Yamamoto announced his plans to the Chief of Staff of the 11th Air Fleet (11th Koku Kantai), Rear Admiral Takijiro Onishi. Together, they considered the capabilities of the aircraft and the distance they would have to travel to strike the ships and return to their mother carriers. They were unable to solve this problem during the discussion, which cooled Onishi's enthusiasm. He suggested Yamamoto that a young officer, Minoru Genda, who believed in the strength and abilities of aviation, could take care of the entire impact plan.

In January 1941, Genda started to work with a great enthusiasm and within a few days, taking into account all the arguments and counterarguments, he prepared a final report for Admiral Onishi. Genda pointed out that the mountains, which cannot be avoided in any way, will be a difficulty and may significantly reduce the chances of success. There were points in Genda's plan that Onishi did not agree with. He believed that American battleships should be the first target, while Genda argued that aircraft carriers should be destroyed first. He believed that air control would be the most important tool of the future war, and a necessary condition for gaining air superiority. That is why the destruction of American aircraft carriers should be done in the first phase.

Genda said a condition for success was the use of 300 aircraft based on six carriers in the expected operation. At that time, the Japanese had only four suitable vessels ("Akagi", "Kaga", "Sōryū", "Hiryū") and had to wait for two more—"Shōkaku" and "Zuikaku"—to enter service. Their construction was being completed at that time. The expected date of their commissioning was set for the summer of 1941. To ensure that the technical staff and aviators would not have problems with operation, the impact plan provided for the planes that were currently in service with the 11th Air Fleet.

In March 1941, Onishi handed over the plan to Genda to be refined, and two months later it was fully completed. Although technical ambiguities were taken into account from the outset, many of them were resolved at the last minute.

Minoru Genda was the creator of the attack plan on Pearl Harbor. [Author's collection]

On April 10, the 1st Air Fleet was formed. At the same time, the 1st Aircraft Carrier Squadron was created, including "Akagi" and "Kaga". The 2nd Aircraft Carrier Squadron was made up of "Sōryū" and "Hiryū". Each division was assigned four destroyers escorts.

There was still no effective solution that would allow torpedoes to be dropped into the shallow waters of Pearl Harbor. Reports from the inspection in Taranto, where it was also shallow, sent by Japanese officers, allowed the commencement of modernization works at the naval arsenal in Yokosuka. The British equipped their torpedoes with wooden stabilizers limiting the depth to which the torpedo dipped after the drop, and the Japanese decided to go the same way. The performed tests and trial drops have shown that the torpedoes used so far dive too deep and need about 200 meters to be armed, therefore they are absolutely not suitable for use in Pearl Harbor.

Another problem was that the Americans used to moor their ships in pairs. The inner battleships were always in a sheltered position and were out of reach for torpedoes. The only way to sink them was to use appropriate bombs, but none of available types were able to penetrate the armour of American ships. Test bombing with 250 kg armour-piercing bombs showed that they were not effective enough, so it was decided to use 409 mm shells used on battleships "Mutsu" and "Nagato". Their adaptation to the new role brought the expected result. A specially designed tail was attached to the projectile, which stabilized its flight. The new 800 kg bomb was capable of penetrating the thickest armour of a Maryland-class battleship, penetrating deep into the ship and causing great damage. It was given the designation Type 99 Number 80 Model 2 and its production started. Tests were carried out at the end of September. The first attempts to bomb the USS "West Virginia" battleship mock-up was carried out by Yokosuka Kokutai's pilots. They were unsuccessful, no hits were obtained. The pilots of the 1st Air Fleet under the command of Mitsuo Fuchida were included in the exercises, but the attempts were also unsuccessful. Only in the following days the mock-up was hit. Based on the experience gained, the most effective method of attacking the target was developed, allowing the destruction of the ship from the ceiling of 3,000 m. It was the minimum allowing the planes to exit the range of anti-aircraft fire.

On August 25, 1941, the 2nd Lt (on October 15 he was promoted to Lt Cdr) Mitsuo Fuchida was transferred to the aircraft carrier "Akagi", where he took command of all air groups of the 1st Air Fleet. Together with Minoru Genda, they trained pilots in Kagoshima Bay for the attack on Pearl Harbor. During the exercises, the problem of torpedoes returned. The pilots were unable to successfully drop them into water shallower than 12 meters, despite the fact that they were equipped with wooden stabilizers. The trials were carried out until the end of September, but they were unsuccessful.

First Aircraft Carrier Squadron consisted of "Akagi" and "Kaga", visible in the photo. Summer 1941 [Author's collection]

"Kaga" aircraft carrier belonged to the 1st Aircraft Squadron together with "Akagi". [Author's collection]

"Hiryū" (pictured) and "Sōryū" were the smallest aircraft carriers involved in the attack on Pearl Hrbor. [Author's collection]

At the end of September, Japanese specialists from the Yokosuka arsenal, conducting experiments on the torpedo stabilizer, managed to achieve their first success. While working on the Model 2 torpedo, they constructed a stabilizer that allowed it to be dropped from the plane onto water 13 m deep. Work continued and in October the new torpedo was ready for service—it was given the designation Type 91 Model 2. Several new solutions were applied, which slightly increased its weight compared to previous models. Wooden stabilizers were installed on the rear part, which increased its chances of being dropped into shallow water. The drop limit was 10 m high for the old ones and 20 m for new torpedoes at a speed not exceeding 160 knots (296 km/h). The minimum distance needed to activate the torpedo fuse was set at 200 m. The depth mechanism was mounted on each copy and made it possible to reduce the depth by 2 m after the drop.

The torpedoes prepared for the attack on Pearl Harbor were highly reliable. All of them had wooden stabilizers mounted on the horizontal and vertical ends of the rudders. They helped it maintain the desired depth immediately after dropping from the plane. After reaching the desired depth, the rudders at the ends of the stabilizers controlled the draft and the course of the torpedo. During the test drops pilots achieved satisfactory results with an approach angle of around 17–20°. If the torpedo was dropped from

"Sōryū" aircraft carrier anchored in the Kuril Islands shortly before the attack on Pearl Harbor. [Author's collection]

Mitsuo Fuchida on August 25, 1941 was transferred to the aircraft carrier "Akagi", where he took command of all air groups of the 1st Air Fleet. [Author's collection]

Arsenal was able to deliver 30 copies by October 15, the second batch of 50 copies by October 31, and the last 100 copies by the end of November. The number of modernized torpedoes delivered to Kogoshima between October 30 and November 4 was sufficient for practical training. The first tests carried out in the bay of 12 m were successful. Over the last few months, the crews of all selected ships have participated in intense exercises in the waters between Kyushu and Okinawa. At the end of October, the planes practiced in two groups over a two-week period. The first of them, consisting of A6M2 fighters, trained in air combat. The second group of B5N2 torpedo bombers and D3A1 dive bombers practiced bombing ground and sea targets. The practice program included training of groups consisting of nine torpedo-bomber aircraft, of which the four best pilots were selected for special training of torpedo groups. These pilots were transferred to the Kagoshima base, where they carried out mock attacks on the anchored ships and exits from the anti-aircraft fire zone in the area of the target. As planned, after take-off, the planes reached a combat ceiling of 2,000 m, after which the key commander in the vicinity of Sakurajima lowered the altitude and flew into the Kotsuki River Valley, simulating the valley between the mountains on the island of Oahu. Over the Iwasakidani Valley simulating the approach from the north to Pearl Harbor base, the ceiling was lowered again to a height of 50 m, and then to 15 m above Kagoshima base, imitating the final approach to the target at Pearl Harbor. Intensive flights were also carried out at night. Pilots were practising night take offs and getting into the formation, as well as torpedo attacks.

too great height, the wooden stabilizers caused it to hit the bottom of the bay. When dropped from the low altitude and high speed of the aircraft, the impact of the torpedo on the water surface limited the deflection of the rudders, which resulted in an unstable torpedo course and the destruction of wooden stabilizers. The pilot had a great responsibility, he had to take into account all elements of the attack and make a proper approach by individually deciding on the drop height. For example, a simple error in assessing the minimum distance from the target could prevent the torpedo warhead from arming.

It turned out that the problem was the timely supply of stabilizers for torpedoes. The

On August 8, 1941, the aircraft carrier "Shōkaku" was commissioned, which accelerated the pace of preparations. After leaving the base in Yokosuka, the carrier sailed to Ariake Bay where it was officially incorporated into the 5th Aircraft Carrier Squadron. Within two months, the pilots assigned to the carrier un-

Type 91 Kai 2 torpedoes aboard the aircraft carrier "Akagi", anchored in Hitokappu Bay in the Kuril Islands shortly before departing to attack on Pearl Harbor. In the background, the "Hiryū" aircraft carrier is visible. [Author's collection]

Aircraft carriers "Zuikaku" (pictured) and "Shōkaku" became part of the 5th Aircraft Carrier Squadron after commissioning. [Author's collection]

Aircraft carrier "Shōkaku" at Yokosuka port several days after commissioning. August 23, 1941 [Author's collection]

derwent training related to deck take offs and landings. "Zuikaku" entered service on September 25. On November 3, aircraft carriers with escort units gathered in Ariake Bay, and the next day a practice attack was carried out similar to the actual conditions of the impact at Pearl Harbor.

Air squadrons, commanded by Lt Cdr Mitsuo Fuchida, grouped on four aircraft carriers ("Shōkaku" and "Zuikaku" did not participate in these exercises) conducted an attack on targets in Kagoshima Bay. The planes took off from the ships at a distance of approximately 370 km (200 nautical miles) and attacked the targets in two waves. The first one hit at 7:00 a.m. and the second at 8:30 a.m. About 20 miles from the target, dive bombers gained altitude and torpedo-bombers lowered it. The target of the attack was the Japanese battleships participating in the manoeuvres. The B5N2 planes armed with torpedoes did not take part in the second wave of the attack, as, according to the assumptions of the exercises, there was no longer any element of surprise. Dive bombers attacked the ships, and at the same time B5N2 struck Saeki airfield. The exercise was completed after 9:00 a.m.

The failure of the torpedo planes during the exercises resulted from the torpedo immersion after dropping too deep, which in the shallow waters of Pearl Harbor could cause them to sink to the bottom of the bay. Looking for a solution to this problem, Lt Cdr Genda flew to Kagoshima for consultations with the pilots of torpedo aircraft. Their aim was to work out ways to limit the submersion of torpedoes and to obtain the maximum number of hits. Two drop methods have been suggested. The first one was to drop torpedo from a height of 20 m at a speed of 100 knots, the second one to do it from a height of 10 m at a speed of 100 knots and with nose of the plane tilted down by 1.5°. The new method was personally tested by the commander of the air base in Kagoshima, Lt Cdr Shogo Masuda (later air officer on "Akagi"), obtaining 80% of hits.

During the meeting of the Imperial Navy Command, which took place on November 4, 1941, a decision was made to start hostilities. On the following day, the Combined Fleet received Order No.1 Daihonei Kaigun Meirei 1-go, and on November 7th, the date of the attack was set for December 8, 1941.

On November 13, 1941, "Akagi" raised the anchors and headed for Kagoshima. Air officers Murata, Fushida and Masuda arrived on board, and in the afternoon Vice Admiral Nagumo with his staff boarded. At the same time, pilots and crews were settling on strike group aircraft carriers. Moving such a large number of personnel from ground bases to ships in a manner imperceptible to American intelligence was a very difficult task and required a schedule. This operation was carried out until November 17, and on the same day all aircraft carriers designated for the Hawaiian operation entered Saeki Bay, where Adm. Yamamoto held a short briefing aboard the "Akagi".

Pilots of the B5N2 torpedo-bombers from the carrier "Kaga" pose for a commemorative photo on board of their ship. December 6, 1941 [Author's collection]

At around 4 p.m., Japanese ships began leaving Saeki Bay and headed for the Kuril Islands. "Hiryū" was first to leave, followed closely by "Sōryū". "Shōkaku" and "Zuikaku". "Akagi" sailed off after darkness. The aircraft carrier "Kaga", before arriving in Saeki, was in the dock of the Sasebo shipyard between November 11 and 14. On November 17, the unit participated in a gathering in Saeki Bay, after which she sailed to Sasebo the same day, where she took on board 100 torpedoes for the strike at Pearl Harbor. Specialists from Yokosuka were also boarded, and they finished modifying the torpedoes on board of the carrier.

Before the strike team began concentrating in Hitokappu Bay in the Kuril Islands, the gunboat "Kunajiri" entered it with orders to completely suspend telegraph and telephone communications between the outside world and the island of Etorofu. This was to keep the gathering of such a large number of ships in secret.

Concentration at the Hitokappu Bay was completed on November 22 at 15:15. "Shōkaku" was the last to arrive. Supply units systematically transferred the necessary supplies to the ships. After the transhipment was completed, they were to remain in the bay until 10 December.

On the morning of November 23, a conference was organized for officers from the various ships involved in the operation. It was opened by Vice Admiral Nagumo, who said: "Your mission is to attack Pearl Harbor." Lieutenant Commander Minoru Genda, who discussed opera-tional details, said the entire attack on the US base would last from half an hour to an hour. The first goal is to destroy battleships and aircraft carriers anchored around Ford Island, and then disperse the air force over Oahu. The attack was to consist of two waves. The first, commanded by Lt Cdr Mitsuo Fuchida, who was also the commander of the entire attack, was to include all types of carrier-based aircraft. About 230 nautical miles north of Oahu, this formation was to take off from aircraft carriers and were scheduled to launch an attack on designated targets around 8:00 a.m. The second wave of the attack was commanded by Capt. Shigekazu Shimazaki. It included fighters, dive bombers and torpedo-bombers, which were to take off from ships 200 nautical miles from Oahu. Its task was to completely destroy the ships damaged by the first wave of the attack, and to completely destroy the enemy aviation. In the event of a possible American counterattack, all B5N2s were to be armed with torpedoes. While the strike team was in the vicinity of Hawaii, the A6M2 fighters and D3A1 dive bombers were to be prepared for take-off from each carrier from sunrise to sunset.

Commanders Genda and Fuchida discussed five possible scenarios of the attack:

—The Pacific Fleet is located at Pearl Harbor;

—The Pacific Fleet is at Lahaina anchorage;

—Part of the Pacific Fleet is at Pearl Harbor and part at Lahaina anchorage;

Concentration of ships assigned to attack Pearl Harbor in Hitokappu Bay was completed on November 22, 1941. The photo shows a view from the "Zuikaku" deck to Hitokappu Bay. [Author's collection]

—The Pacific Fleet is at sea and the strike forces will meet it on the way;

—The Pacific Fleet is at sea and the strike force will not meet it.

The discussion focused primarily on the first option. According to its assumptions, the first wave attack should start around 8:00 a.m. The formation of 189 aircraft was to include 50 B5N2 torpedo-bombers armed with bombs and commanded by Lt Cdr Fuchida, 40 B5N2 torpedo-bombers armed with torpedoes under the command of Lt Shigeharu Murata, 54 D3A1 dive bombers commanded by Lt Cdr Kakuichi Takahashi and 45 A6M2 fighters commanded by Lt Cdr Shigeru Itaya.

The first to attack the battleships and air-craft carriers was Lt Cdr Murata leading the group of B5N2 armed with torpedoes. Lt Cdr Fuchida leading the B5N2s with bombs was to attack the battleships around Ford Island. Dive bombers were to focus on attacking Wheeler and Hickam bases. The fighters should cover their own formation and, after destroying the enemy planes, attack Wheeler, Hickam, Kaneohe and Barbers Point bases.

The second wave of attack was to take off from carriers an hour after the first wave. When flying at operating speed, it should reach the target approximately half an hour after the first wave completes its attack. It was not supposed to include B5N2 planes armed with torpedoes because if the first wave had failed the surprise attack, the strike of the torpedo-armed planes could have brought large losses with little damage to enemy ships. The formation of 171 planes was consisting of 54 bomb-armed B5N2s, commanded by Capt. Shigeharu Shimazaki (their task was to attack Hickam, Kaneohe and Ford Islands airfields), 81 D3A1 dive bombers under the command of 2nd Lt Takashige Egusa (attack on ships anchored at Pearl Harbor), and 36 A6M2 fighters under the command of Capt. Saburo Shindo,

View from the "Akagi" deck of the ships anchored in the Hitokappu Bay. November 23, 1941. [Author's collection]

View from the deck of "Zuikaku" towards the "Kaga" sailing in front of it on the way to Hawaii. Note the barrels of the 127 mm AA artillery. [Author's collection]

which were to attack Wheeler, Kaneohe, Hickam and Ford Island after the complete destruction of the airborne enemy.

The attack plan assumed that all 40 B5N2s armed with torpedoes would attack simultane-

Capt. Shigekazu Shimazaki aboard the "Zuikaku" aircraft carrier. This officer led the second wave of the attack on Pearl Harbor. [Author's collection]

ously. According to this, planes should be divided into two strike groups. After separation, the first group under the command of 2nd Lt Murata, consisting of two formations of 12 planes, was to continue south, bypass Oahu from the east and reach the point at the entrance to the canal. Then it would change course to the north and, going towards Hickam Field, strike the battleships in one or two raids. The attack on the battleships should be carried out by groups of three to five planes. The second-strike group, which included two formations of eight planes, was commanded by Capt. Nagai. Their task was to sink American aircraft carriers from the northwest and west. Commander Murata feared that the attack plan would change, and the dive bombers would strike first. The smoke and clouds of fire after first attack could make it very difficult to drop the torpedoes accurately.

A very important problem related to the torpedo attack was the issue of installing anti-torpedo nets around American ships. The intelligence data transferred to the "Akagi" in Hitokap Bay did not mention anything about it, nor was it possible to determine whether the enemy had installed them or was in the process of being installed. So far, there was no solution to this issue. Checking the possibility of cutting the net by torpedoes, carried out by specialists in Yokosuka, also did not bring results. The problem was serious, so during the conversation with Vice Admiral Nagumo, Fuchida suggested

**Organization of Nakajima B5N2 attack groups of the first wave of attack on Pearl Harbor according to the order of November 24, 1941**

| Classification | | Commander | | Amount | Target |
|---|---|---|---|---|---|
| First group | First Strike Group | Commander of air group from "Akagi" | Commander of air group from "Akagi" | 15 B5N2s from "Akagi" | Main target – battleships Secondary target – aircraft carriers, heavy cruisers, other warships in close vicinity |
| | Second Strike Group | | Commander of air group from "Kaga" | 15 B5N2s from "Kaga" | |
| Second group | Third Strike Group | Commander of air group from "Hiryū" | Escadrille commander from "Sōryū" | 10 B5N2s from "Sōryū" | Main target – battleships, aircraft carriers Secondary target –heavy cruisers, other warships in close vicinity |
| | Fourth Strike Group | | Commander of air group from "Hiryū" | 10 B5N2s from "Hiryū" | |
| Third special group | First Special Strike Group | Commander of formation from "Akagi" | Commander of formation from "Akagi" | 12 B5N2s from "Akagi" | Main target – battleships, aircraft carriers Secondary target –heavy cruisers, other warships in close vicinity |
| | Second Special Strike Group | | Commander of formation from "Kaga" | 12 B5N2s from "Kaga" | |
| | Third Special Strike Group | | Escadrille commander from "Sōryū" | 8 B5N2s from "Sōryū" | |
| | Fourth Special Strike Group | | Escadrille commander from "Hiryū" | 8 B5N2s from "Hiryū" | |

that the first plane from the attacking formation could suicidally hit the net, tearing it apart with its load. Should the first plane miss, the next one will try the same. Nagumo had doubts, but Fuchida dispelled them, claiming that despite the technical difficulties, the pilots would complete the task. Aviation personnel who were acquainted with this proposal were obliged to maintain secrecy, and the pilots began to look for their own solutions to this problem.

On November 26, 1941, at 6:00 a.m., in complete darkness, all ships of the strike team under the command of Vice Admiral Nagumo raised their anchors and began to slowly leave Hitokap Bay. At 09:00, the formation of the combat group began, and then the navigation through the North Pacific. On December 6 (Hawaiian time), it reached a point of 600 nautical miles north of Oahu. At 11.30 a.m. the ships changed course to the south and increased their speed to 20 knots. On December 7 (Hawaiian time), information about the lack of barrage balloons and anti-torpedo nets around American ships came from Japanese intelligence officer Yoshikawa. However, the last intelligence report that reached the Japanese before the attack was not so favourable—it said that American carriers had left Pearl Harbor.

## Tora! Tora! Tora!

Punctually at 1:30 a.m. (6:00 Hawaiian time) on December 8, 1941, at 230 nautical miles from Oahu, planes of first wave of attack took off. (Describing the attack on Pearl Harbor, au-

Nakajima B5N2 takes off from the deck of a Japanese carrier. [Author's collection]

The first wave of B5N2 takes off from the deck of the "Zuikaku" aircraft carrier to attack Pearl Harbor. [Author's collection]

thor decided to quote two times in parallel: Tokyo time as first, and Hawaiian time as second. Due to the geographical shift of time zones, there are differences in determining the date of the attack on Pearl Harbor: in Hawaii it was December 7, and such date is given in English publications. In Japan it was December 8, and such date is mentioned in Japanese texts). Shortly after taking off of the initial wave, mechanics began to prepare the second group.

After the concentration was completed, the pilots began to form the combat formation. Commander of the first wave—which took off from "Akagi"—was the commander of the entire formation, Lt Cdr Mitsuo Fuchida, who led his 1st Strike Group. It consisted of three escadrilles, consisted of two flights each:
—1st escadrille: flights 40, 41 (5 aircraft),
—2nd escadrille: flights 42, 43 (5 aircraft),
—3rd escadrille: flights 44, 45 (5 aircraft).

Two hundred meters behind it, the 2nd Strike Group, which took-off from "Kaga", set its position in column. The group was led by 2nd Lt Takashi Hashigushi. This formation also included three escadrilles with two flights each:
—1st escadrille: flights 40, 49 (5 aircraft),

B5N2 torpedo bombers launched from "Shōkaku" to attack Pearl Harbor. A frame from the Japanese film chronicle. [Author's collection]

B5N2 (BII-307) of the 4th Strike Group taking off from "Hiryū", carrying an 800 kg armour-piercing bomb. [Kagero Archive]

—2nd escadrille: flights 47, 48 (5 aircraft),
—3rd escadrille: flights 43, 46 (4 aircraft).

Third position in column, at a distance of 500 m, was taken by the 4th Strike Group which was launched from "Hiryū". It was commanded by 2nd Lt Toshio Hashimoto, and it consisted of two escadrilles:
— 1st escadrille: flights 40, 48 (5 aircraft),
—2nd escadrille: flights 46, 47 (5 aircraft).

At the end of the column, at a distance of 200 m from the previous groups, flew the 3rd Strike Group, taking off from the aircraft carrier "Sōryū". The formation was led by 2nd Lt Sadao Yamamoto. It also had two escadrilles:
— 1st escadrille: flights 1, 2 (5 aircraft),
—2nd escadrille: flights 1, 2 (5 aircraft).

The entire column consisted of bomb armed B5N2s and flew in a central formation line at an altitude of approximately 3,340 m.

On the right, 500 m from the Fuchida strike group, was a Special Strike Group under the command of 2nd Lt Shigeharu Murata. The 1st Special Assault Group from the "Akagi" consisted of two escadrilles:
— 1st escadrille: flights 46, 47 (6 aircraft),
—2nd escadrille: flights 48, 49 (6 aircraft).
Behind it, successive special groups formed in a column at equal distances from each other (200 m).

The 2nd Special Strike Group from "Kaga" aircraft carrier, commanded by Capt. Kazuyoshi Kitajima, consisted of two escadrilles:
— 1st escadrille: flights 41, 44 (6 aircraft),
—2nd escadrille: flights 44, 45 (6 aircraft).
Next was the 3rd Special Strike Group from the aircraft carrier "Sōryū", under the command of Capt. Tutomu Nagai. It was composed of two escadrilles:
— 1st escadrille: flights 1, 2 (4 aircraft),
—2nd escadrille: flights 1, 2 (4 aircraft).

The column was closed by the 4th Special Strike Group from "Hiryū", commanded by Capt. Heita Matumura and consisting of two escadrilles:
— 1st escadrille: flights 40, 41 (4 aircraft),
—2nd escadrille: flights 42, 43 (4 aircraft).

All B5N2 from special groups were armed with torpedoes and flew at an altitude of approximately 3,100 m.

On the left side of the Fuchida's column, at an altitude of 3,700 m, flew a formation of D3A1 dive bombers under the command of 2nd Lt Kakuichi Takahasi. Escort fighters, led by 2nd Lt Shigeru Itaya, took position over the formation at an altitude of 4,800 m.

Under the direct command of Lt Cdr Fuchida there were 89 B5N2 torpedo-bombers in total (40 armed with torpedoes and 49 bombs), 51 D3A1 dive bombers and 43 A6M2 fighters. The entire formation consisted of 183 planes.

Punctually at 2:45 a.m. (7:15), 200 nautical miles from Oahu, the second-strike group started from carriers. Take offs were completed at 3.00 a.m. (7:30). After formation of the battle array, the group flew towards the target. The leading aircraft was piloted by the commander of the entire formation, 2nd Lt Shigekazu Shimazaki with his 6th Strike Group, which took-off from "Zuikaku". It consisted of three escadrilles:
— 1st escadrille: flights 41, 42, 43 (9 aircraft),
—2nd escadrille: flights 45, 46, 47 (9 aircraft),
—3rd escadrille: flights 51, 52, 53 (9 aircraft).

Five hundred meters behind them, the 5th Strike Group from "Shōkaku" took its position in formation. It was commanded by Capt. Tutomu Hagiwara and consisting of three escadrilles:
— 1st escadrille: flights 41, 42, 43 (9 aircraft),
—2nd escadrille: flights 45, 46, 47 (9 aircraft),
—3rd escadrille: flights 50, 51, 52 (9 aircraft).

The entire B5N2 formation was armed with bombs and flew at an altitude of about 3,000 m in the central line of the formation. On the right, 1,000 m from the 5th Strike Group, flew

B5N2 (AI-301) plane from the "Akagi" aircraft carrier. Cdr. Lt. Mitsuo Fuchida took part in the attack on Pearl Harbor piloting this plane. The photo was taken during the Indian Ocean raid.
[Author's collection]

the beginning of a column of four D3A1 attack groups led by 2nd Lt Takashi Egusa. Cover fighters under the command of Capt. Saburo Shindo, took positions in front of the entire formation, on the left side of the B5N2 group and over the whole group at an altitude of 3,500 m. Under the direct command of 2nd Lt Shigekazu Shimazaki flew 54 B5N2 torpedo-bombers, 78 D3A1 dive bombers and 35 A6M2 fighters—167 machines in total.

At 3:10 a.m. (7:40), upon reaching the northern tip of Oahu (Kahuku Point), Fuchida ordered his pilots to take an attack position. B5N2 from the first and second group commanded by Fuchida (armed with bombs) continued their flight at an altitude of 3,000 m. Shigeheru Murata's B5N2s armed with torpedoes lowered the flight altitude. As the planes neared the target, the morning light brightened the scene, reveal-

ing the ships at Pearl Harbor, which now could be clearly seen. Unfortunately, the American aircraft carriers that should be the target for 16 torpedo bombers from "Sōryū" and "Hiryū" were not among them. It was expected that they would enter the port on the night of December 6 to 7 (Hawaiian time), but this did not happen.

Northwest of the Ewa Field airfield, the torpedo-bombers split into two formations. The first of them consisted of two strike groups commanded by Capt. Tutomu Nagai and Capt. Heita Matumura. It headed towards the Middle Loch (west side of Ford Island). The second formation also consisted of two groups under the command of 2nd Lt Shigeharu Murata and Capt. Kazuyoshi Kitajama. The torpedo-armed planes flew southeast, then turned north and northwest, and in a long arc

B5N2 (AI-301) of 1st Strike Group. The plane was piloted by Capt. Matuzaki (navigator—Fuchida, machine gunner—Mizuki). The photo was taken during the Indian Ocean raid.
[Author's collection]

B5N2 from the aircraft carrier "Akagi" flying at low altitude. [Author's collection]

past Hickam Field, then they headed toward the line of battleships.

At the same time 2nd Lt Shigekazu Shimazaki, who commanded the second wave of the attack, was halfway to Oahu with his 167 aircraft.

## Torpedo-armed B5N2 operations

As the first at Pearl Harbor were planes from "Hiryū", under the command of Capt. Matamura, followed by machines from "Sōryū" commanded by Capt. Nagai. From the Middle Loch, they attacked ships anchored on the west side of Ford Island. Before the attack,

Capt. The Nagai distributed the targets among the individual planes, and all pilots were explicitly ordered to attack targets, even at the cost of their own lives.

The first attack was commenced by three aircraft of "Sōryū" group. Their target was the light cruiser USS "Raleigh" (CL-7) moored at berth F-12, and the target ship USS "Utah" (AG-16) at berth F-11. At 3:26 a.m. (7:56), planes flying in the Pearl City axis began the attack. The machine piloted by Capt. Nakajima (navigator—Nakamura, machine gunner—Nishida) attacked the USS "Utah". The torpedo was dropped at around 3:26 a.m. (7:56) and hit the ship in the area of frame 58. The explosion of the torpedo broke the hull plating from frame 55 to frame

Fifty four B5N2s (all armed with bombs) took part in the second wave of the attack. [Author's collection]

| Classification | Commander (commander of the whole raid— Lt Cdr Shigekazu Shimazaki) | | Amount |
|---|---|---|---|
| 5th Strike Group | Capt Tutomu Hagiwara | 1st escadrille | 9 aircraft |
| | | 2nd escadrille | 9 aircraft |
| | | 3rd escadrille | 9 aircraft |
| 6th Strike Group | Lt Cdr Shigekazu Shimazaki | 1st escadrille | 9 aircraft |
| | | 2nd escadrille | 9 aircraft |
| | | 3rd escadrille | 9 aircraft |

**Organization of Nakajima B5N2 attack groups of the second wave of attack on Pearl Harbor according to the order of November 24, 1941**

61 and damaged the fuel tanks. Through the resulting breach, water broke into the hull and made the ship tilt to the port side.

The light cruiser USS "Raleigh" was attacked by P/O Sato (navigator—Sema, machine gunner—Arai). The torpedo swam at a depth of 4 m and hit the cruiser exactly at the height of the turret and frame 58. The explosion damaged the shell plating on the ship's sides from frames 50 to 60, which resulted in flooding the internal compartments and the ship's slow inclination to the port side.

The third American ship—the USS "Detroit" (CL-8) light cruiser—was attacked by P/O Harada (navigator—Kanai, machine gunner—Hosoi), who dropped the torpedo at 3:30 a.m. (8:00 a.m.). Unfortunately, it was not accurate, and it swam 23 meters aft of the cruiser (between the USS "Detroit" and USS "Raleigh" cruisers), and then sank at the bottom of the bay on the western part of Ford Island.

After the first surprise passed, cruisers and destroyers anchored on the roadstead of the East Loch opened the AA fire.

Immediately after that, the second formation from "Sōryū", consisting of three aircraft, attacked. P/O Fujihara (navigator—Yuii, machine gunner—Natahien) hit USS "Utah". The explosion of the torpedo tore the plating from frames 77–82, flooded the inner spaces of the hull and became the direct cause of sinking the

ship. "Utah" dramatically increased her lean to 15° port. Commander of the ship, 2nd Lt Squith, who was replacing the absent commander, made the decision to abandon the vessel. At 8:05 a.m. the ship increased lean to 40°, and after another five minutes—to 80°. At 8:12 a.m. she capsized.

B5N2 piloted by P/O Kawajima (navigator—Tanaka, machine gunner—Okawa) attacked USS "Raleigh", while P/O Kimura (navigator—Yoshioka, machine gunner—Wakamiya) hit USS "Detroit". Both torpedoes missed the ships and buried in mud at the bottom of the bay on the eastern side of Ford Island. Around 3:35 a.m. (8:05) the USS "Releigh" began to increase its bank dangerously and, on the orders of the commander, counter-ballasting was started to prevent the ship from overturning.

The crews of torpedo-bombers had to act under very difficult conditions, as the pilots attacked the ships under the bright morning sun. Another reason for the failure was the effective anti-aircraft fire from cruisers and destroyers. At this critical moment, Capt. Nagai made the decision to change goals. His two planes, and the entire 4th Special Strike Group from "Hiryū", consisting of eight planes, under the command of Capt. Matumura, flew over Ford Island in search of targets "worthy" of attack.

The bomb run on ships anchored on the western side of Ford Island lasted about 10–12

**Nakajima B5N2 (EII-307) from the "Zuikaku" during the flight over Hickam Airport (second attack wave). The plane was piloted by P/O Kawada. Crew: navigator—Kaneda, machine gunner—Shinoda. [Author's collection]**

Nakajima B5N2 (EII-307) from the aircraft carrier "Zuikaku" at Pearl Harbor. [Author's collection]

Lieutenant Ichiro Kitajima informs the crews of Nakajima B5N2 *Kate* aboard aircraft carrier "Kaga" about the plan to attack Pearl Harbor. December 6, 1941 [Author's collection]

American battleships at Pearl Harbor as seen from one of the Japanese planes during the attack. [Author's collection]

minutes. At the same time, the PBY *Catalina* flying boats base on Ford Island was attacked too.

The torpedo planes, which found themselves in the further part of the bay, in the area of Dry Dock No. 1 and Dry Dock No. 2, saw the battleship USS "Pennsylvania" anchored there, but the closed dock made it impossible to drop torpedoes directly. The Capt. Nagai's attention was drew by ships tied to each other side to side at Wharf 1010, where the USS "Pennsylvania" would normally dock, so he decided to attack the heavy cruiser of the Portland class spotted there.

The first attack was carried by Capt. Nagai (navigator—Soichiro Taniguchi, machine gunner—Goro Ota). The dropped torpedo swam at a depth of 6 m and passed under the bottom of the USS "Oglala" (CM-4) minelayer and exploded at 3:27 a.m. (7:57) after hitting the light cruiser's USS "Helena" (CL-50) hull. The USS "Oglala" was tied to the port side of the USS "Helena". The torpedo hit just below the armoured belt at the height of the engine room, at a depth of about 6 m. The explosion tore the outer plating of the hull over a considerable space—from frame 69.5 to frame 80.5. The explosion was so strong that it broke the outer plating of the port side of the USS "Oglala", which caused it to sink later.

Right after Capt. Nagai his attack commenced P/O Yanagimoto (navigator—Yumoto, machine gunner—Matuo). The torpedo he dropped got stuck in the mud and detonated for unknown reasons.

The second raid on the moored ships was carried out by a formation of three B5N2s from "Hiryū" armed with torpedoes. After drop the torpedoes probably sailed too deep and passed under the bottom of the ships, and then around 3:28 a.m. (7:58) they exploded at the wharf. The attack was difficult, pilots were blinded by the sun's rays reflected from water.

Six torpedo planes were approaching from the east in Southeast Bay over Merry Point. Above the bay, the machines lowered the ceiling to 15 m above the water and headed towards the battleships. The 4th escadrille from "Akagi" targeted the battleship USS "Oklahoma" (BB-37). The attack on the ship was started by the commander of the 47th flight, Lt Zinichi Goto. The USS "Oklahoma" was tied to the outer port side of the USS "Maryland" battleship. The first torpedo was dropped in its direction at 3:33 a.m. (8:03) from the plane flown by Lt Zinichi Goto (navigator—Mitsuo Miyajima, machine gunner—Masutoshi Meda). It hit frame 64, about 6 m below the waterline. The explosion ripped most of the outer torpedo bubble and bent the inner plating of the hull.

The second torpedo dropped from the plane piloted by St. Kotami (navigator—Miyata, machine gunner—Onata) at 3:33 a.m. (8:03), hit frame 47.5, also 6 m below the waterline. Its explosion caused similar damage as the first torpedo. The outer plating of the anti-torpedo bubble was torn, and the inner plating of the hull was damaged. Both of these hits made the ship tilt to port. The third plane was piloted by St. Yasuke (navigator—Hayato, machine gunner—Hagitami). While approaching the drop zone, he came under heavy anti-aircraft fire from battleships and the pilot had to drop the torpedo at

the wrong angle. It passed under the bottom of the USS "Oklahoma" and hit the pole-support of the mooring berth. The plane was heavily shot (21 hits were later counted), although it managed to return to the mother carrier.

The third torpedo to hit the USS "Oklahoma" was dropped from a plane piloted by P/O Shigeo Suzuki (navigator—Haruyoshi Shigenaga, machine gunner—Seinosuke Minaki) at 3:36 a.m. (8:06), it struck the frame 63, very close to the edge of the side armour.

At 3:36 a.m. (8:06) a torpedo was dropped from a B5N2 piloted by P/O Tadehara (navigator—Matuoka, machine gunner—Nakamura). It swam towards the battleship and hit its frame 67 near the end of the armoured belt. The explosion smashed half of the lower edge of the inner lane several meters long. This resulted in a gap approximately 13 cm wide in the armoured segment between the upper edge of the plate near frame 67 and the lower edge near frame 70. As a result of the explosion of four torpedoes, the armoured belt was dented inside to a depth of several centimetres. Large amount of water penetrated into the hull, which caused the ship to lean to the port side. The growing

tilt was the reason why the torpedoes hit higher and higher parts of the hull.

The fifth torpedo that hit the ship was dropped at 3:36 a.m. (8:06) from the plane piloted by P/O Itsuda (navigator—Sano, machine gunner—Nakano). It struck halfway up the side armour, close to frame 56. Another torpedo for the USS "Oklahoma" was dropped by Capt. Kitajima Kazuyoshi (navigator—Akiwaki Yutaka, machine gunner—Yamamoto Shizuo). It hit exactly halfway up the armour belt on frame 53, and its explosion caused further internal damage to the hull.

At 3:36 a.m. (8:08), the formation of three B5N2s from the "Kaga" carrier began the attack on the battleship. Another (seventh) torpedo was dropped from the plane piloted by P/O Yoshiro Yoshikawa (navigator—Ohjino Koji, machine gunner—Maeda), which struck near the main mast, above the middle of the armoured belt, near frame 89. The explosion of the warhead caused a breach in the plating an external anti-torpedo bubble 14 m long and 10 m high, and a slight distortion of the side armour. P/O Hirata (navigator—Yamaguhi, machine gunner Suzuki) missed the target.

The sunken USS "Oglala". [Author's collection]

Photo taken from a Japanese plane on December 7, 1941 showing the beginning of the attack on American battleships at Pearl Harbor. [Author's collection]

Nakajima B5N2 torpedo-bombers from "Zuikaku" in flight over Pearl Harbor. [Author's collection]

The eighth torpedo that hit the battleship was dropped at 3:39 a.m. (8:09) by Capt. Matumuru Heita (navigator—Shiro Takeo, machine gunner—Murao Sadamu) from "Hiryū". It hit half of the upper armour belt near frame 42. The explosion torn the light outer skin of the hull above the armour belt and deformed the 11.5 m long side plating by 5.5 m. The armoured belt was bent inwards to a depth of several centimetres.

The last torpedo that hit the USS "Oklahoma" was dropped around 3:40 a.m. (8:10) from a plane flown by P/O Ohis (navigator—Kokuro, machine gunner—Inake). It hit the ship at the deck level in the vicinity of frame 55. The vessel was tilted about 35–40° to port at that time. Detonation of the warhead torn the side plating 12 m long and 13 m high and caused the greatest damage to the interior of the hull. Water forced its way inside through the gaps, flooding other rooms on the port side. The ship leaned her left anti-heel keel against the bottom of the bay. There was only 3 m between the bottom of the ship and the bottom of the bay, so the ship could not overturn, but the tilt gradually increased until USS "Oklahoma" rested the superstructures on the bottom of the bay.

Almost simultaneously aircraft from the "Akagi" carrier attacked the battleship USS "West

Sunk destroyers USS "Cassin" and USS "Downes", and the battleship USS "Pennsylvania" in Dry Dock No. 1 after the attack. [Author's collection]

Virginia" moored to the port side of the USS "Tennessee". The attack was led by the commander of the 46th flight of 4th escadrille— Lt Cdr Shigeharu Murata (navigator—Yoji Hoshino, machine gunner—Kiyoshi Hirayama). At 3:33 a.m. (8:03) he dropped a torpedo which hit the side armour about 1 meter from the edge of the armour belt. The explosion pushed the armour inwards to a depth of 20 cm. The hull plating under the belt has been internally ripped and completely squashed. The damage caused the fuel leakage from the port outer tanks.

The second torpedo, which hit the ship, was dropped from a plane piloted by P/O Fukuji Murakami (navigator—Zensaku Kawamura, machine gunner—Kaneo Fujimoto). It hit the side armour between frames 79–80, exploding about 1.5 m from the lower edge of the belt. The wa-

ter violently burst in and shattered the outer skin under the armour belt, causing the ship to slowly tilt to the port side.

Third torpedo was dropped at 3:33 a.m. (8:03) from a plane flown by P/O Kokawa (navigator—Risuta, machine gunner—Tamoyasu) and hit the lower part of the armour at frame 92, about 2 m from the upper edge of the belt. The explosion dented the plating and the lower half of the side armour to a depth of 25 cm. The tilt increased so much that only a quick counterbalancing prevented the ship from overturning.

The fourth torpedo was dropped at 3:36 a.m. (8:06) by P/O Nakazawa (navigator—Fukuda, machine gunner—Onishi). It hit half of the lower side armour, at the junction of two armoured segments, near frame 70. The explosion destroyed the outer plating of the hull

B5N2 (EI-311) from the aircraft carrier "Shōkaku" participated in the second wave of the attack on Pearl Harbor. The planes attacked the Kaneohe Bay Marine Air Station. [Author's collection]

The B5N2 from the aircraft carrier "Shōkaku"departs from Kaneohe Bay after bombing. [Author's collection]

under the armour belt. For a distance of about 12 m, the bent sheets of the plating protruded downwards.

At 3:38 a.m. (8:08) the fifth torpedo was dropped from a plane piloted by P/O Nakazawa (navigator—Yoshino, machine gunner—Kanasaki). It swam at a depth of 6 m and hit the rudder near the frame 145. The explosion threw it outside and destroyed the steering gear compartment.

The sixth torpedo was dropped by P/O Hirotake Inata (navigator—Hidgo Morisaki, machine gunner—Seiichiro Hirano). It hit the battleship at 3:39 a.m. (8:09) halfway up the armour in the area of frame 68. As a result of this and previous hits in this part of the ship, the armour belt was dented to a depth of 60 cm and its upper part moved from frame 67 to 72, also, between frames 63 and 71, the armour was completely destroyed.

The seventh torpedo which hit the battleship USS "West Virginia" was dropped by a B5N2 from "Kaga", flown by P/O Shigekatu Onashi (navigator—Yoshizo Masuda, machine gunner—Hidemi Takeda). It struck exactly below the armour belt in the vicinity of frame 81. The force of the explosion pushed the side armour inwards to a depth of about 20 cm and

destroyed the hull plating above the armour belt at a length of about 8 m. Internal rooms in this area were also damaged.

The eighth torpedo was dropped from the plane piloted by Capt. Hiroharu Kakuno (navigator—Masaji Inada, machine gunner—Yutaka Morita) from the "Hiryū" aircraft carrier. At 3:40 a.m. (8:10) it hit the hull of the ship at the height of frame 94, and the explosion dented the plating above the armoured belt inwards.

The last, ninth torpedo to hit the USS "West Virginia" was dropped by P/O Sugimoto (navigator—Maruyama, machine gunner—Fujiyama). It struck the battleship's port side when it was about 28–30° tilted to the port. The torpedo entered through breaches and damaged the outer plating of the hull above the armour belt near frame 68. Explosion erupted exactly below the second armoured deck, causing significant damage, followed by an explosion of 127 mm ammunition. The hull outer plating was damaged from frame 62 to 100.

At 3:36 a.m. (8:06) B5N2 aircraft from "Akagi" attacked the battleship USS "California" moored to quay F-3. The first torpedo was dropped from a machine piloted by Capt. Kokishi (navigator—Kawamura, machine gunner—Kiyomizu). It swam at a depth of 4 m and hit

the port side of the ship near frame 97.5. The explosion of the warhead cut a 9 m long and 5.5 m high breach in the hull, burst the internal fuel tanks in this area and initiated an explosion of battleship's ammunition magazines.

The second torpedo was dropped by P/O Umito (navigator—Ito, machine gunner—Horii) and it hit the ship in the vicinity of frame 53. The explosion tore the hull plating 10 m long and 5.5 m high and cracked the fuel tanks causing leakage. Both the first and second torpedoes that hit the USS "California" detonated on the thin plating, directly under the side ar-

mour strip. Explosions caused the water to penetrate deep into the hull, as a result of which the ship slowly sank and landed at the bottom of the bay.

Third plane from the carrier "Kaga", flown by P/O Kitahara (navigator—Shimizu, machine gunner—Onishi), was under heavy anti-aircraft fire while approaching the drop zone and the pilot released the torpedo at the wrong angle, as a result of which it passed by USS "California" and got stuck in mud. The plane was hit multiple times and caught fire, then crashed at the Naval Hospital. The navigator jumped out of

**Hull of the sunken battleship USS "Oklahoma" protruding from the water. [Author's collection]**

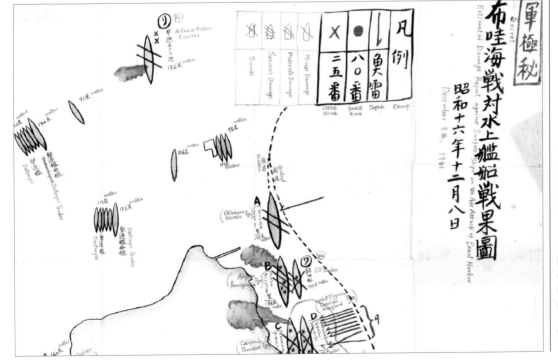

**Fragment of a map with the damage assessment caused by the attack on Pearl Harbor, prepared by Lt Cdr Mitsuo Fuchida, who was introduced to Emperor Hirohito. [Author's collection]**

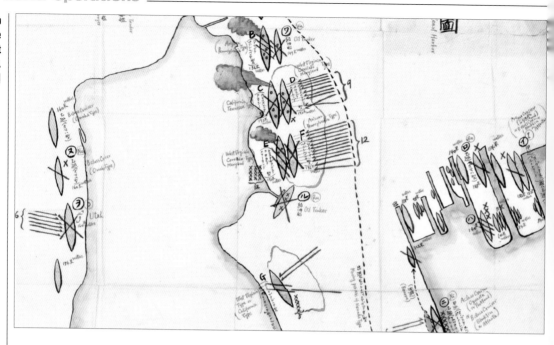

Another fragment of the map with an assessment of the damage sustained as a result of the attack on Pearl Harbor. [Author's collection]

The bay-bottomed battleships USS "West Virginia" (BB-46) and USS "Tennessee" (BB-43) photographed the day after the attack. [Author's collection]

the flaming machine without a parachute and landed next to the USS "New Orleans". He was picked up from water, but the following day he died of injuries. The pilot and the guinner died in the wreckage of the crashed machine.

At 3:38 a.m. (8:08) the "Akagi" torpedo formation completed their attack on American battleships and began regrouping before returning to the mother carrier.

In the literature, there are information about a torpedo which hit the battleship USS "Arizona", based on reports from the USS "Vestal" (AR-4) workshop ship moored to the port side of "Arizona". In 1943, the sludge was pumped out from the bottom of the ship, but divers penetrating the port forward section of the hull, below the turret barbet in the torpedo bubbles, found no damage from the torpedo. The existing damage in the vicinity of the fore turret No. 1 has been identified as a result of an 800 kg bomb explosion at close range. Based on these findings, it can

The sunken USS "California" (BB-44) the day after the attack on Pearl Harbor. [Author's collection]

Part of a B5N2 wing from the aircraft carrier "Kaga" (AII-35...?), which crashed near the Naval Hospital as a result of damage from anti-aircraft artillery fire during the attack on the battleship USS "California". [Author's collection]

Extinguishing the fires on the USS "Nevada". During the attack the ship was hit, among others, by one torpedo. [Author's collection]

Burning battleships USS "West Virginia" and USS "Tennessee". [Author's collection]

be concluded that the USS "Arizona" was not torpedoed.

At 3:32 a.m. (8:02), the battleship USS "Nevada", moored to the F-8 quay, opened the machine gun fire at the incoming torpedo planes commanded by Capt. Kazuyoshi Kitajima flying with his 41st flight from the "Kaga". One of the pilots from this group, P/O Tanaka (navigator—Namura, machine gunner—Okami), dropped a torpedo towards the battleship, which swam

at a depth of 7 m and directly at 3:33 a.m. (8:03) exploded on the port side of the vessel, between the bow turrets, near frame 41, about 4.2 m above the keel. The explosion of the warhead ripped a large 4.8 m long and 8.22 m high hole in the torpedo bubble. The explosion caused the outer plating and the double bottom plating to bend over a distance of 7.5 m, from frame 37 to 43. The anti-torpedo bulkhead became concave at the double bottom. Water began to

flood the rooms below the first deck level on port side, between frames 30–43, and the ship slowly started to lean for 5°, but counterbalancing reduced the tilt almost to zero.

At 3:40 a.m. (8:10) the torpedo planes of the first strike wave completed their attack and having reported to the Commander-in-Chief by radio, headed to the concentration point.

Shortly after 3:35 a.m. (8:05) Lt Cdr Fuchida, waiting with his bomb armed B5N2 group, gave the order to attack. Two machines joined them. During the first raid on the targets, the pilots were greeted by strong anti-aircraft fire, which prevented an effective attack.

The 2nd escadrille commanded by Capt. Goro Iwasaki and the 3rd escadrille under the com-

**Sunken, burning wreck of the USS "Arizona" after ammunition magazines exploded. [Author's collection]**

**Ammunition explosion on destroyer USS "Shaw". The stern of the USS "Nevada" is visible on the right. [Author's collection]**

At Kaneohe air base, which was attacked by B5N2 aircraft, among others, 27 PBY *Catalina* flying boats were completely destroyed and a further 6 were damaged. [Author's collection]

Nakajima B5N2 (AII-356) wreck from the "Kaga" aircraft carrier. It was flown by Capt. Mitumori Suzuki (crew: Morita Tunenori, Kazunori Tanaka). Wreckage excavated from the bottom of the southern Pearl Harbor bay. [Author's collection]

mand of Capt. I. Furukawa from the aircraft carrier "Akagi" had a better luck. The attack carried out by them at 3:40 a.m. (8:10) on the battleship USS "Tennessee" ended up with two direct hits. The first bomb exploded directly on the armoured roof of turret No. 3, and the second hit the middle cannon of turret No. 2. An explosion on the roof of the turret started a fire in its vicinity.

The attack was continued by B5N2s from the "Kaga" aircraft carrier under the command of 2nd Lt Takahashi Hashiguschi. The first escadrille hit the battleships USS "Maryland" and USS "West Virginia" at 3:38 a.m. (8:08). The latter was struck by two bombs and the ship began to lean to the port side. The first bomb hit the top of the front mast and penetrated two decks of the combat deck. It passed through the superstructure and the main deck around frame 70 and exploded on the second deck on the port side. The explosion caused very severe damage between frames 65–75, tearing off a large area of the port side and demolishing rooms on the first and second decks. This hit increased the dam-

**Nakajima B5N2 Kate losses during the attack on Pearl Harbor**

| No. | Attack wave | Ship | Unit | Crew |
|-----|-------------|------|------|------|
| 1 | First wave | "Kaga" | 1st escadrille 44th flight | Osami Kitahara, Yoshio Shimizu, Toshio Onishi |
| 2 | First wave | "Kaga" | 2nd escadrille 44th flight | Mitsumori Suzuki, Tsuneki Morita, Kazunori Tanaka |
| 3 | First wave | "Kaga" | 2nd escadrille 44th flight | Kenichi Kumamoto, Isamu Matsuda, Nobuo Umetsu |
| 4 | First wave | "Kaga" | 2nd escadrille 45th flight | Shigekatu Ohashi, Yoshio Masuda, Hidemi Takeda |
| 5 | First wave | "Kaga" | 2nd escadrille 45th flight | Izumi Nagai, Yoshiharu Machimoto, Tomoharu Takeda |

age that had previously been caused by the ninth torpedo's explosion.

The second bomb fell directly on the roof of the main artillery tower No. 3, but for unknown reasons it did not explode. However, it completely destroyed two seaplanes located there. The burning fuel that leaked from the planes caused a fire, which was quickly extinguished.

The second escadrille from the "Kaga" carrier, led by Capt. Maki, attacked the USS "Arizona" moored at the F-7 quay at 3:44 a.m. (8:14). One of the first bombs exploded between turrets No. 1 and No. 2, above the gunpowder storage. The blast of the explosion hit through the open hatch and caused an explosion that was the direct cause of blowing up the ammunition chambers. Another bomb struck near the command post, in front of the main mast, and the blast damaged its load-bearing structure. The falling mast crushed the superstructure and leaned against the forward command post. After the ammunition explosion, the fire began to spread, fuelled by fuel leaking from the damaged tanks.

Capt. Sadao Yamamoto from "Sōryū", flew unexpectedly over the USS "Nevada", which, despite severe damage, was still afloat. The artillerymen from the ship immediately opened fire to the approaching plane, and perhaps that is why there was no direct hit.

"Akagi's" 1st escadrille under the command of Lt Cdr Fuchida made a second attempt to attack the line of battleships at 3:47 a.m. (8:17). The attack resulted in two direct hits to the fore deck of the USS "Maryland" battleship. The bomb explosions destroyed and bent the deck plating and ripped out many small holes in the vicinity of frame 13.

At 3:59 a.m. (8:29), Fichida—the raid commander—gave the radio order to terminate the attack and proceed to the designated concentration points before returning to the carriers.

The second wave of the attack on Pearl Harbor involved B5N2s armed only with bombs. The group took-off from "Shōkaku" at 4:30 a.m. (9:00) and attacked Kaneohe airbase, along with A6M2 fighters. Most of the bombs fell on hangar No. 1, but also hangar No. 3 was hit. The planes standing outside the hangars were

B5N2 pilot Lt. Jinichi Goto of the "Akagi" aircraft carrier. [Author's collection]

destroyed. Twenty seven of 33 PBY *Catalina* flying boats based in Kaneohe were completely destroyed and the remaining 6 were damaged.

Eighteen B5N2s under the command of Capt. Hagiwara hit targets on Ford Island, where they came under heavy anti-aircraft fire from ships. After completing the task, they flew to the concentration area before returning to their mother carriers.

The second wave bombers caused much damage on land and further damage to the ships. The attack was completed at 5:15 (9:45).

During the attack on Pearl Harbor, five Nakajima B5N2 *Kate* torpedo bombers were lost and another 10 were damaged.

## Combat operations in Southeast Asia

At almost the same time as the 1st Air Fleet's planes attacked Pearl Harbor, other Japanese forces attacked American bases in the Philippines. The main burden of combat operations fell on land-based air units there, however, to attack targets beyond the range of land planes, it was decided to use the 4th Aircraft Carrier Squadron, which at that time included only

Two Nakajima B5N2 torpedo-bombers in flight. Mount Fuji is seen at the background. [Author's collection]

In January 1942, Nakajima B5N2s were used in various combat operations. [Author's collection]

a small "Ryūjō" carrier. The ship had 18 B5N2s torpedo-bombers on board, as well as 15 A5M4 *Claude* fighters.

On December 7, 1941, 13 B5N2s commanded by Capt. Aioi and escorted by nine fighters took-off from "Ryūjō". The target was the port of Mindanao, but the raid did not bring any effect, although it was not without losses. One B5N2 was shot down by AA defence, and the other had to land on its way back due to damage. The B5N2 from "Ryūjō" on the same day attacked Mindanao again, but this time it was commenced only by two bombers, escorted by three fighters. Again, the effects of the attack were negligible and one A5M4 was lost. For the next few days, the B5N2s from "Ryūjō" were used only for reconnaissance flights. On Decem-

ber 12, when the landing on the Legaspi began, they were used to a limited extent to support the land forces.

On December 20, the 1st Aircraft Carrier Squadron, which had meanwhile returned from Hawaii, was directed to the vicinity of Wake Atoll, with the task of supporting the landing on this island. It was fiercely defended by the marines and three F4F *Wildcat* fighters from VMF-211. On December 21, B5N2s from aircraft carriers "Sōryū" and "Hiryū" bombed the island without visible results and returned to their ships unharmed. The next raid of 33 B5N2s was sent to attack the American fortifications on Wake. The Japanese were attacked by two F4Fs piloted by Lt Thornton and Capt. Freuler. By surprise, they quickly shot down two B5N2s, but when the A6M2 escorts joined the action, the Americans did not stand a chance and were quickly shot down. Wake defenders capitulated on December 23.

In January 1942, the 1st and 5th Aircraft Squadrons took part in actions aimed at the capture of New Ireland and New Britain. Air raids on New Guinea were also conducted. From January 20, B5N from "Akagi", "Kaga", "Shōkaku" and "Zuikaku" participated in all these activities. On January 25, aircraft of 2nd Aircraft Carrier Squadron took part in air raids on Celebes. The enemy (RAAF) most often did not have modern equipment in this area and its counteraction in all the above-mentioned operations was negligible, so the Japanese losses were minimal.

Almost simultaneously with the start of the Java landing, on February 19, 1942, 81 B5N2s from "Akagi", "Kaga", "Sōryū" and "Hiryū" aircraft carriers, along with 71 D3A1 dive bombers and 18 A6M2 fighters, attacked Darwin Harbor

The first Japanese air raid on Darwin Harbor took place on February 19, 1942. Note the bright cloud of smoke from the explosion on the ship "Neptune" and dark one from a burning oil pipeline. In the foreground, the corvette "Deloraine" is seen, which escaped damage. [Public domain]

in northern Australia. Convoys with supplies for Australian troops stationed in Java were sent from this port, so it was a very important target for the Japanese. No torpedoes were used in this raid and all B5N2s were used as horizontal bombers. Destroyer USS "Peary", several other ships, and the port infrastructure were destroyed, which made it impossible to supply Java for several months. Over the port, escort fighters quickly shot down a lone P-40E. The Japanese formation headed to the nearby airport from which another five P-40s were taking off, which were also shot down. During the raid, the Japanese lost one B5N2, one A6M2 and two D3A1s, and 34 other planes were damaged. An hour after the deck aircraft attack on Darwin Harbor, G3M2 and G4M1 bombers of 21st and 23rd Koku Sentai from Ambon and Kendari bases completed the destruction.

## Raid to the Indian Ocean

A big operation, in which the Nakajima B5N2 torpedo-bombers played a major role, was the Japanese raid against naval and air bases in the Ceylon region at the Indian Ocean. Its target was the relatively strong Eastern Fleet commanded by Vice Admiral Somerville which included aircraft carriers HMS "Indomitable", HMS "Formidable" and HMS "Hermes" with 94 aircraft on board: 37 fighters (12 Fairey *Fulmar*, 16 Grumman *Martlet*, 9 Hawker *Sea Hurricane*) and 57 (according to other sources—60) outdated torpedo-bombers (45 Fairey *Albacore* and 12 Fairey *Swordfish*). In addition to aircraft carriers, Eastern Fleet included battleships: HMS "Warspite", HMS "Resolution", HMS "Royal Sovereign", HMS "Ramillies" and HMS "Revenge"; heavy cruisers: HMS "Cornwall"

and HMS "Dorsetshire"; light cruisers: HMS "Emerald", HMS "Enterprise", HMS "Caledon", HMS "Dragon", and HMS "Dutch Tromp"; as well as 15 destroyers and 30 smaller ships. About 150 aircraft were stationed at RAF and FAA bases in Colombo, China Bay and Koggala anchorage, most of which were 54 *Hurricanes* Mk. I and Mk. IIb in three RAF squadrons (30th and 258th in Colombo, and 261st in Trincomalee), 40 FAA *Fulmars*, and 14 *Blenheims* from 11th Squadron RAF. There were also outdated Vickers *Vincent* and *Vildebeest*, or Fairey *Seal*. Considering the fact that most of the ships were also outdated (to put it mildly), despite their numbers, the operational value of the British forces in the area was not very great.

The Japanese Imperial Navy directed two groups of ships against Allied group. Strike Force led by Chuichi Nagumo, consisting of the 1st Aircraft Carrier Squadron ("Akagi"), 2nd Aircraft Carrier Squadron ("Sōryū", "Hiryū"), 5th Aircraft Carrier Division ("Shōkaku", "Zuikaku"), battleships "Kongo", "Haruna", "Hiei" and "Kirishima", heavy cruisers "Tone" and "Chikuma", light cruiser "Abukuma", and 8 destroyers. Formation left the Kendari base on March 26, 1942, and entered the Indian Ocean on April 1.

The group of ships commanded by Jisaburo Ozawa consisted of the 4th Aircraft Division ("Ryūjō" aircraft carrier, heavy cruisers "Chōkai", "Kumano", "Mikuma", "Mogami" and "Suzuya", light cruiser "Yura", submarines I-2, I-3, I-4, I-6, I-7, and destroyers "Fubuki", "Shirayuki" and "Hatsuyuki" (until April 3), and from April 4 destroyers "Amagiri", "Asagiri", "Yugiri", and "Shirakumo".

There was a total of 370 aircraft on board of the carriers: 143 B5N2s, 114 D3A1s and 113 A6M2s (there are also other data in the litera-

The deck of one of the Japanese carriers assigned to the Indian Ocean raid, photographed in March 1942 near the island of Celebes. Two more aircraft carriers and other ships can be seen in the background. [Author's collection]

B5N2 take off for the Ceylon raid. A frame from the Japanese chronicle, which was probably taken on the "Akagi". It shows the AI-301 machine piloted by Lt. Fuchida. [Author's collection]

ture, according to which it was a total of 369, 377, or even 396 aircraft). Both the planes and the Japanese ships were much more modern than the British vessels, so the attackers undoubtedly had a technical and numerical advantage, too. The entire Japanese force was commanded by a Vice Admiral Nagumo.

The plan assumed attacking on April 4, 1942, but due to some delays, the operation began the next day. At dawn on April 5, 53 B5N2 bombers under the command of Lt Cdr Fuchida, 38 D3A1s and 36 A6M2 fighters took off from the decks of Japanese aircraft carriers. The first destination of this armada was the port and airports in the Colombo area. The British detected the incoming planes with the help of radars, but not all fighters manage to scramble on time and the A6M2s tied them up in combat. Thanks to this, the B5N2 easily reached the port, where, despite the ordered evacuation, were still about 35 vessels, most of which were merchant ships.

Of the larger units, the auxiliary cruiser HMS "Hector" and the destroyer HMS "Tenedos" were sunk with bombs. Japanese losses in this raid were limited to one A6M2 and seven D3A1s which were shot down by *Hurricanes* and *Fulmars*. The British losses were much more serious. Even before the bombing began, A6M2 fighters from "Hiryū" shot down 6 *Swordfish*, and later the 21 *Hurricanes* and 4 *Fulmars*.

When to Vice Admiral Nagumo began to receive radio reports from the planes involved in the attack on Colombo, he realized that the main forces of the British Eastern Fleet had to be warned earlier, and it fled to the open sea. Intensive searches by reconnaissance planes from the cruiser "Tone" resulted in the detection of two large ships. The pilot recognized them as battleships or cruisers. Wasting no time and without waiting for other planes to confirm the message, around noon, aircraft carriers "Akagi", "Sōryū" and "Hiryū" began launching the aircraft, which were to be a reserve and did not participate in the morning raid. Fifty-three D3A1 dive bombers quickly sank both vessels (HMS "Cornwall" was hit by fifteen 250 kg bombs, and HMS "Dorsetshire" was struck by fourteen). After that the Japanese left Ceylon for two days, fearing a counterattack by the British fleet and aviation. The search for the Japanese force was unsuccessful and on April 8, Somerville ordered his ships to return to anchorage in the Addu area. But the real struggle was yet to come.

On April 9, 1942, the Japanese group again approached Ceylon and at 6:00 a.m., when the ships were already about 100 nautical miles from Trincomalee, 91 B5N2 bombers led by Lt

Cdr Fuchida and 45 A6M2 fighters led by Lt Cdr Itaya took off from carriers. After getting into the formation, they headed towards the port and Trincomalee airport. As before, despite the radar indications, the British fighters did not take off on time and did not manage to prevent the bombing of the port installations and anchoring ships. But this time the British did not suffer major losses. Only the HMS "Erebus" auxiliary monitor and the HMS "Sagaing" ship were sunk. The flight of *Hurricanes* of RAF 261 Squadron attacked the A6M2 formation from the "Zuikaku", and both sides lost two planes as a result of the fight. The British attacked B5N2s when the bombs were already dropped, but they immediately were furiously attacked by the A6M2 escort fighters. Nine *Hurricanes*, two B5N2s and three A6M2s were shot down as a result of the dogfight that broke out over the port.

While the raid on Trincomalee was in progress, a reconnaissance seaplane from cruiser "Haruna" detected the carrier HMS "Hermes" escorted by three destroyers. The situation from three days ago repeated, and without further thinking, the Vice Admiral Nagumo ordered the remaining D3A1 dive bombers to take off. Eighty-five *Vals*, led by Lt Cdr Egusa, and nine A6M2 fighters started for their mission.

First, at 10:23 a.m., HMS "Hermes" was located by the D3A1s from "Shōkaku" and the order to attack was immediately given. The aircraft carrier HMS "Hermes", together with its escorting destroyer HMS "Vampire", corvette HMS "Hollyhock" and the auxiliary ship HMS "Althelstone" were sunk so quickly that the D3A1 from "Sōryū", which arrived on place as

Another chronicle's frame showing the start of the B5N2 from the "Akagi" aircraft carrier during the Japanese raid to the Indian Ocean. [Author's collection]

Same situation as on previous photograph. The plane is armed with bombs. [Author's collection]

British carrier HMS "Hermes" was sunk on April 9, 1942 by Japanese Aichi D3A1 *Val* dive bombers. [Author's collection]

Nakajima B5N2 from the "Akagi" aircraft carrier in flight over the target. Japanese raid to the Indian Ocean, April 1942 [Author's collection]

During the Indian Ocean raid, the B5N2 planes performed really well. [Author's collection]

last group, found no targets for themselves and eventually attacked a convoy of three ships, two of which—the tanker S/S "British Sergeant" and the freighter S/S "Norvikien"—were sank. Shortly after the end of the attack on the HMS "Hermes", *Fulmars* of FAA 273 Squadron arrived to cover it. They came too late but managed to shoot down three D3A1s and damage another three. Eight *Fulmars* of FAA Squadron 803 and 806 attacked D3A1s from "Sōryū", left without a fighter escort, but they took the fight and turned out to be a formidable opponent. After about half an hour of combat, two British planes and four *Val* bombers perished in the waters of the Indian Ocean.

When the raid on Trincomalee continued and the D3A1 bombers were approaching HMS "Hermes", unexpectedly over the ships of the Vice Admiral Nagumo's group flew nine British Bristol *Blenheim* bombers from RAF 11th Squadron. The surprise was complete, but the bombs dropped from a height of 3,000 m only framed the aircraft carrier "Akagi" and the cruiser "Tone", with no direct hits. On the way back, the British formation was intercepted, first by the patrolling A6M2, and later by the returning aircraft from "Hiryū" and "Shōkaku". As a result, six *Blenheims* were shot down. Fearing of further attacks by British aviation, although there was no loss, the Vice Admiral Nagumo considered

B5N2 with torpedo takes off from the deck of the "Zuikaku" aircraft carrier. Battle of the Coral Sea, May 4–8, 1942. [Author's collection]

B5N2 lands on the "Shōkaku" aircraft carrier. Battle at the Coral Sea, May 4–8, 1942. [Author's collection]

the operation completed and decided to withdraw his forces. This decision may be controversial today due to being overly cautious.

There is no doubt that in this phase of the war, the D3A1 dive bombers proved to be an extremely effective weapon against enemy ships, and the B5N2 fulfilled their role as horizontal bombers, too.

Parallel to the activities of the Vice Admiral Nagumo's Strike Force, was operating the small group led by Vice Admiral Ozawa. This force included, among others, small aircraft carrier "Ryūjō" with 15 B5N2s and 12 A6M2s on board. Planes were actually dealing only with enemy transport ships and were quite successful. During the Indian Ocean raid, they sank 19 vessels with a total displacement of 100,000 BRT.

## Battle in the Coral Sea

Another target of the Japanese offensive was Port Moresby. Its control would make it possible to occupy all of New Guinea in a short time, and from here it was only one step to the invasion of Australia. The Port Moresby was one of the most important ports and communication hubs of the Allies in this area. The operation against this base was codenamed MO. To carry it out, a group of forces led by Rear Admiral Aritomo Goto were separated, including three aircraft carriers: "Shōkaku" and "Zuikaku" (5th Aircraft Carrier Squadron commanded by Vice Admiral Takeo Takagi), and a small aircraft carrier "Shōhō". Before attacking Port Moresby, it was necessary to capture the island of Tulagi, where the Japanese landed on May 3, 1942. The landing went smoothly and was successful, but

on the next day Japanese troops were bombed by deck bombers from the American carrier USS "Yorktown", which—on the orders of Admiral Nimitz—secretly arrived in the area. The Japanese did not know anything about it, and the news of the appearance of the American carrier reached the Vice Admiral Takagi with a considerable delay. USS "Lexington" joined USS "Yorktown" on May 6, thus forming the Task Force 17 (TS-17). These events marked the beginning of the preparations for both sides of the first aircraft carrier duel in this war, which went down in history as the Battle of the Coral Sea. Both sides frantically tried to locate the enemy forces by sending numerous reconnaissance planes.

On May 7, 1942, around 8:00 a.m., a strike group consisting of 36 D3A1 dive bombers led by Lt Cdr Takahaschi and Capt. Ema, 26 B5N2 torpedo bombers led by Capt. Shimazaki and Capt. Ichichara, and 18 A6M2 escort fighters took off from "Shōkaku" and "Zuikaku" carriers. The formation was sent against the vessels detected by reconnaissance aircraft and identified as aircraft carrier and cruiser. It quickly turned out that the detected targets were in fact the American tanker USS "Neosho" and destroyer USS "Sims", but it was too late to abort the action. In this situation, the B5N2 and A6M2 were sent back, and the dive bombers attacked. The destroyer was sunk, and the tanker was badly damaged. One D3A1 from "Zuikaku" was hit by anti-aircraft fire and crashed into the ship's deck.

The Japanese group was temporarily left without any aircraft capable of striking enemy ships and would again become a poorly defended target in the event of an attack by American bomber and torpedo planes. Luckily for the

Burning USS "Lexington" after crew abandoned the ship. Battle of the Coral Sea. May 8, 1942. [Author's collection]

B5N2 take off from a Japanese carrier. During the Battle of the Coral Sea, two torpedoes dropped by these planes hit the USS "Lexington". [Author's collection]

Japanese, the American equivalent of a Vice Admiral Takagi—Rear Admiral Fletcher—also sent his planes not over Japanese carriers, but over the counterattack invasion force led by Rear Admiral Goto. The only carrier in that group was "Shōhō". It became an easy prey and was quickly sunk by planes from USS "Lexington" and USS "Yorktown".

On the same day, at 4:30 p.m., after refuelling and rearming, 12 D3A1s and 15 B5N2s from aircraft carriers "Shōkaku" and "Zuikaku", once again took off with the task of attacking the detected USS "Lexington". The Japanese did not manage to achieve their goal because the Americans detected them with radar and sent four F4F fighters commanded by Capt. Remsey, quickly supported by more machines of this type from USS "Lexington". The *Wildcats* shot down 9 B5N2 and D3A1, and another *Val* was shot down by the AA artillery. On the way back,

11 Japanese machines did not find their own carriers and fell into the water due to lack of fuel, so only 6 machines returned from action. The loss 21 aircraft with experienced crews was a very painful blow for the Japanese, especially that the decisive battle was yet to come.

On May 8, at around 9:00 a.m., all combat-capable Japanese planes (18 B5N2s, 33 D3A1s and 18 A6M2s) under the command of Lt Cdr Takahashi headed towards the detected USS "Lexington" and USS "Yorktown". American carriers also launched their air groups, which in turn took the course for the Japanese ships. Strike group led by Lt Cdr Takahashi was the first to arrive at the target. The Japanese intended to apply their classic tactic of attacking in two phases, first were B5N2 torpedo bombers commanded by 2nd Lt Shimazaki, and immediately after them (practically in parallel)—D3A1 dive bombers. The Japanese did not have the

forces to attack both American aircraft carriers simultaneously, so USS "Lexington" was the primary target. The first attack of the B5N2 was unsuccessful since already during the approach to the target three machines were shot down by the *Wildcats*, and the dropped torpedoes passed the ship from starboard and port side (three each). At the same time, at a distance of 650 meters from the aircraft carrier, three B5N2s led by Capt. Ichohara dropped their torpedoes. Two of them reached the target. The first hit the amidships and the second struck the bow. Meanwhile, four B5N2s led by Capt. Sato attacked the USS "Yorktown" aircraft carrier, but none of the torpedoes hit the target. Two aircraft were shot down. After the torpedo attack, dive bombers joined the action. Fourteen machines from "Zuikaku" struck USS "Yorktown", and 19 more attacked USS "Lexington". The accuracy of the bomb drops left much to be desired, but three of them hit the target and caused damage so severe that it ultimately sank USS "Lexington". Two more bombs hit USS "Yorktown", but in this case there were only fires which the ship's crew quickly seized.

At almost the same time the surviving Japanese planes set out on their return course, their mother ships were attacked by the Americans. The aircraft carrier "Shōkaku" was hit by three bombs and excluded from combat. During the battle, the Japanese lost 17 D3A1s, 13 B5N2s and 4 A6M2s, including planes that failed to land on their own ships due to lack of fuel.

## Midway

The Battle of Midway, which began on June 4, 1943, ended with a tactical and strategic victory for the Americans. Also, the tactical initiative was then reclaimed by the US forces.

The American base on Midway Atoll was an important strategic point, but its capture was not a goal itself for the Japanese. First of all, it was still believed that such an attack would force the American Pacific fleet to counteract, and it would be possible to defeat it in a general battle. The Japanese wanted to lure out and destroy the aircraft carriers that were considered the greatest threat. Initially, the plans of Admiral Isoroku Yamamoto related to the operation encountered strong resistance from the Naval General Staff and the Imperial Army, but opposition ceased after April 18, 1942, when Lt Col James Doolittle successfully raided Tokyo with B-25 bombers launched from the carrier. This attack was a one-off action and caused only minor damage but had a large psychological ef-

Aerial view of Midway Atoll, November 24, 1941. The Japanese seizure of this island would have been last step before the invasion of Hawaii itself. [Author's collection]

Nakajima B5N2 *Kate* played an important role in the Battle of Midway. [Author's collection]

An armour-piercing bomb with a mass of 800 kg under the B5N2 fuselage. [Author's collection]

fect. The Japanese realized that they were not safe even on their home islands, and the Americans had some success in the end.

The Japanese quickly realized the seriousness of the threat of American aircraft carriers, knowing from where the Doolittle B-25s must have taken off from (the thesis found in older literature saying that the Japanese believed the B-25s flew from Midway is not true). The surprise of the Doolittle's attack resulted in putting maximum strategic priority on destroying the enemy aircraft carriers, and Yamamoto-proposed operation against Midway provided such an opportunity. In addition, the capture of this atoll would significantly increase the range of Japanese air reconnaissance, thus hindering further American raids. Moreover, after the capture of Wake, the landing on Midway was the last step before the invasion of Hawaii itself, the seizure of which would push the Pacific Fleet as far as the US West Coast and give Japan a free hand in its operations in the Western Pacific. The

prospects were extremely tempting, and in this context, the Naval General Staff accepted Yamamoto's plans. The Imperial Army also agreed without further opposition to allocate the appropriate forces for the invasion of Midway.

The Battle of the Coral Sea did not settle anything and ended in a tactical draw, without affecting the further plans of the Japanese, who were still striving to fight a decisive battle and destroy the enemy fleet, and the impending invasion of Midway seemed to provide an excellent opportunity for this. At the same time, it was planned to carry out a diversionary operation against the Aleuts, which was to tie some of the American forces, but as the future showed, this multiplicity of targets was to be the weakest side of the Japanese plan.

The plan to seize Midway, codenamed MI (Yamamoto himself was appointed commander of the entire operation), was approved on April 5, 1942. The Japanese failed to keep it secret. US intelligence had broken the code used by the Imperial Navy, and US Pacific Fleet head-quarters had time to prepare for what was to come. Three large aircraft carriers have arrived to Midway: USS "Enterprise", USS "Hornet" and USS "Yorktown" (which was repaired after the Battle of the Coral Sea). Besides, the tiny island itself was literally crammed with planes and all the materials necessary for the aviation operations. The decisive clash that the Japanese were so keen for was inevitable this time.

The Japanese forces assigned to take part in the MI operation included the 1st Aircraft Carrier Strike Team, commanded by the Vice Admiral Chuichi Nagumo, the main force's security team led by Admiral Isoroku Yamamoto, and the invasion group to take Midway under the command of the Vice Admiral Nobutake Kondo. The back-bone of 1st Assault Team were four large aircraft carriers: "Akagi", "Kaga", "Sōryū" and "Hiryū". In addition, it included two high-speed battleships ("Haruna" and "Kirishima"), two heavy cruisers ("Tone" and "Chikuma"), 12 destroyers and 5 oil tankers.

The security group consisted of seven battleships (including "Yamato"), the "Hōshō" light aircraft carrier, two seaplane transporters, two light cruisers, and twelve destroyers. Of these, four battleships and two cruisers were assigned to cover the Aleutian operation, in which the main role was to be played by the 2nd Strike Team consisting of two carriers: "Ryūjō" and

"Junyo". It was assumed that after completing the task, these ships were to take part in the expected decisive battle with the Pacific Fleet intervening after the attack on Midway.

The invasion force was divided into groups: covering, fire support, amphibious assault and support. In addition to the transporters, it included two high-speed battleships, eight heavy cruisers and destroyers.

Fourteen submarines were deployed on the expected approach courses of the Pacific Fleet sailing from Pearl Harbor towards Midway and the Aleutians. Another submarine—I-168—operated in the Midway area.

Nakajima B5N2 taking off from an aircraft carrier. [Author's collection]

Two B5N2 *Kate* from "Hiryū" aircraft carrier fly over the USS "Yorktown" after dropping torpedoes. Note the numerous explosions of AA artillery shells. [Author's collection]

Damaged B5N2 flying over the waves. Many of these machines, along with experienced crews, were lost in the Battle of Midway. [Author's collection]

Nakajima B5N2 in flight over the "Sōryū" aircraft carrier. The machine is most likely preparing to land, as evidenced by the dropped hook. [Author's collection]

In total, the Japanese had 322 deck planes at their disposal. Of these, 227 aircraft were on board of the aircraft carriers of the 1st Strike Team (including 21 more for the forces that were to be stationed on Midway in the future) and practically they constituted the Japanese strike force in the upcoming battle.

American forces under the command of Rear Admiral Frank J. Fletcher were divided into two Task Forces. TF-16 commanded by Rear Admiral Raymond A. Spruance consisted of USS "Enterprise" and USS "Hornet" carriers, five heavy cruisers, an anti-aircraft cruiser, nine destroyers, and four oil tankers for ships. The second team—TF-17—commanded by a Rear Admiral Fletcher consisted of USS "Yorktown" carrier, which was repaired after damage sustained during the Battle of the Coral Sea, and two heavy cruisers plus six destroyers.

In total, the Americans had 233 deck aircraft. In addition, on Midway were stationing 17 B-17 *Flying Fortress* heavy bombers, 6 Grumman

TBF *Avenger* torpedo bombers, 4 Martin B-26 *Marauder* bombers, 19 Douglas SBD *Dauntless* dive bombers, 21 Vought SB2U *Vindicatar* dive bombers, 21 Brewster F2A *Buffalo* fighters, 7 Grumman F4F *Wildcat* fighters and 31 Consolidated PBY *Catalina* reconnaissance flying boats (126 machines in total).

On June 4, 1942, at 4:30 in the morning, 108 aircraft (36 B5N2s, 36 D3A1s and 36 A6M2s) commanded by Capt. Tomonaga, formed an array, and set towards Midway. Their task was to bomb the military installations on the island. The USMC F4F *Wildcat* and F-2A *Buffalo* fighters of VMF-221 Squadron took off to intercept the incoming formation, but they failed to stop the Japanese. The manoeuvrable and fast A6M2 quickly dealt with the Americans, and the bombers hit selected targets on Midway without major problems. However, the airfield and other important targets were not destroyed. During the bombing run four B5N2s, one D3A1 and two A6M2s were lost. Capt. Tomonaga reported that the raid had not given the expected result and should be repeated.

At the same time, Vice Admiral Nagumo was awaiting reports from previously dispatched reconnaissance seaplanes and did not yet know that there were three American carriers nearby, which had departed from Pearl Harbor after receiving the information about the Japanese force's approach. Since Nagumo did not get any information from the scouts about the enemy's appearance, he agreed to Tomonaga's suggestion and ordered to rearm the reserve bombers—originally prepared for the attack on American ships—with fragmentation bombs and prepared them for the next raid on the island. So far, everything has gone as expected by the Japanese. Although the attacks from Midway bombers and

Right main landing gear
leg and engine cowling
of Nakajima B5N2 *Kate*.
[Author's collection]

torpedo planes still had to be fought off, their effectiveness was none, and the losses of the Americans were large. At 7:28, a report was received from the last of the sent scouts. Observers form the seaplane from the "Tone" cruiser reported the detection of several large American ships but did not mention the carriers. After a few reminders for a specific identification from the seaplane, a report stated: "The enemy group consists of five cruisers and five destroyers". The news was reassuring, but Nagumo ordered the recce planes to be sent again. Such an operation took a long time, because they had to be lifted below the deck and prepared for the next flight there. In a hurry, the fragmentation bombs re- moved from the planes were placed against the hangar walls without wasting time taking them to the storage. As it turned out later, the consequences of that action were disastrous. At 8:20 a.m. another report was received from the reconnaissance seaplane, in which there was an information about one aircraft carrier in addition to the previously mentioned ships. A moment later this information was confirmed with the addition of two more ships. Vice Admiral Nagumo already knew that he had found the backbone of the American forces, but still did not realize that the enemy had three aircraft carriers, and that their SBD *Dauntless* dive bombers were on their way to the Japanese group.

B5N2 from an unknown unit. 1942–1943 [Author's collection]

Around 10:20 a.m. Nagumo ordered a strike group to take off to destroy the detected aircraft carrier. Japanese ships turned to the wind in preparation for this operation, but at that moment American dive bombers appeared and immediately attacked. The surprise was complete, and the Americans quickly managed to eliminate three aircraft carriers from the fight. "Akagi", "Kaga" and "Sōryū" were hit directly several times. Japanese planes were standing on the deck ready for take off and were completely destroyed. Vice Admiral Nagumo only had one aircraft carrier left—"Hiryū"—with 37 aircraft ready for action. It was not a force that could seriously threaten the American Task Force, but it was still dangerous.

These group took off at 11:00 a.m. and their target was USS "Yorktown". The first to arrive were D3A1s under the command of Capt. Kobayashi, however, they fell under the fire of the F4F *Wildcats* patrolling the area. Only seven machines broke into the ship—the rest were shot down. Three most experienced pilots claimed direct hits, but three more were shot down by the AA fire. The American aircraft carrier was damaged so badly that its speed

dropped to 6 knots, but thanks to the efforts of the repair crews, after an hour, the speed was increased to about 20 knots. It was not the end of the fight because at 14:30, USS "Yorktown's" radar operators detected unidentified planes approaching. As it turned out, these were the remaining 9 B5N2s from "Hiryū", and one surviving machine from "Akagi". The formation was led by Capt. Tomonaga. According to orders, target for these planes were not the USS "Yorktown", but the first undamaged American aircraft carrier encountered (the Japanese already knew about the presence of three American ships of this class), but Tomonaga divided his formation into two groups of five aircraft and ordered to attack USS "Yorktown" from two sides instead. The Japanese once again received heavy AA fire from ship's artillery. Also, the US fighters were very active in defence. First victim was Tomonaga himself, shot down by Lt Tchach, the commander of the VF-3, who had just taken-off from the attacked carrier. Tomonaga released the torpedo and right after that burst into the water in flames.

Five B5N2s were shot down, but two other dropped torpedoes which hit the ship, causing it to roll 26°, which forced the carrier's boilers to be extinguished. The crew abandoned the ship, and planes from USS "Yorktown" landed on the USS "Enterprise" and USS "Hornet".

When the surviving planes returned to "Hiryū" and their refuelling and rearming began, SBD *Dauntless* of VB-3, VB-6 and VB-8 Squadrons appeared over the last operational aircraft carrier of 1st Air Fleet. Americans attacked in waves and finally sank the ship.

The Imperial Navy suffered the first devastating defeat in this war. Four large aircraft carriers were lost. Two hundred fifty-seven aircraft were destroyed, including 44 shot down in air combat. The most painful and difficult loss,

B5N2 takes off for a combat mission. [Author's collection]

however, was the death of so many experienced crews. The Americans lost the USS "Yorktown" and 148 aircraft.

Simultaneously with the dramatic events on Midway, the Japanese launched a diversionary attack on the Aleutian Islands in which two small aircraft carriers—"Junyo" and "Ryūjō"—took part. Both vessels carried 21 B5N2s, 24 D3A1s and 32 A6M2s on their decks. Their actions were limited to attacking bases and airports in Dutch Harbor, but due to bad weather and enemy air force counteractions, they turned out to be ineffective. The fight ceased on June 4, 1942. The Japanese lost 11 aircraft during this battle: 3 B5N2s, 4 D3A1s, 3 A6M2s and one reconnaissance seaplane.

## Solomon Islands, New Guinea, Rabaul

After the lost battle the Japanese navy reorganized its structure. The 1st Fleet was renamed the 3rd Fleet consisting of 1st ("Shōkaku", "Zuikaku" and "Zuihō") and 2nd ("Ryūjō", "Junyo" and "Hiyō") Aircraft Carrier Squadron. A total of 300 aircraft were stationed on their decks, and the basic strike force was still D3A1 dive bombers and B5N2 bombers.

In August 1942, the priority of the Imperial Navy was to recapture Guadalcanal from the Americans and take control of the entire Solomons. The operation to recapture the island was codenamed KA and was to be carried out by the Shock Team under the command of Vice Admiral Nagumo. Among others, it should include "Shōkaku" and "Zuikaku" aircraft carriers. It was supposed to cover a group of transporters led by Rear Admiral Raizo Tanaki, set to

drop off the ground forces on Guadalcanal to strengthen the Japanese garrison, already heavily bleeding out in the battles with the Americans. Nagumo's aircraft carriers should cover the landing of troops, and in the event of the appearance of American aircraft carriers—to neutralize them. A total of 142 aircraft were stationed on "Zuikaku" and "Shōkaku" (54 D3A1s, 36 B5N2s and 52 A6M2s). In addition, a small aircraft carrier "Ryujō" with 9 B5N2s and 23 A6M2s on board was also assigned to destroy Handerson airfield at Guadalcanal and distract attention by causing an American attack. Three US aircraft carriers were designated to operate against the Japanese forces: USS "Saratoga", USS "Enterprise" and USS "Wasp", but the latter was sent from the Solomon Islands area shortly before the battle to replenish supplies and fuel.

On August 23, 1942, six B5N2s armed with bombs took off from "Ryujō" to bomb Handerson airfield. They were accompanied by fifteen A6M2s, six of which acted as fighter cover, while other nine were assigned to assault the airfield with on-board weapons.

As the Japanese formation approached the island, "Ryujō" was detected by the Americans. In order to attack it, the air special group was launched form "Saratoga" aircraft carrier. Japanese planes after bombing the Handerson Field were attacked by the F4F USMC and P-400 of the 67th Fighter Squadron. Three B5N2s and three A6M2s were shot down, and a four B5N2s were seriously damaged and had to land at ocean.

During the fight over the airport, "Ryujō" was attacked by SBD *Dauntless* dive bombers from "Saratoga". Three of the bombs hit the ship directly, and three more exploded close to its sides. Only one of the torpedoes dropped by

B5N2 armed with a torpedo just before take off for the next combat mission. [Author's collection]

B5N2 landing on the aircraft carrier "Zuikaku". Battle of Santa Cruz Island, October 1942 [Author's collection]

Americans examine the captured B5N2. The photo was taken after the war. [Author's collection]

first Japanese planes reached their destination, it turned out that plenty of American fighters is already hovering over their ships providing air cover. A6M2 engaged some of the *Wildcats*, and the bombers began the attack. The USS "Enterprise", which was attacked by 18 D3A1 dive bombers, was chosen as the first target. The ship was hit by three bombs, the explosions of which blocked the rudder, tilted the vessel several degrees, and started numerous fires. The situation was brought under control only after 18:30, however, it must be admitted that she was quite lucky, because her defensive capabilities were very limited, and the planes of the second wave of the attack did not find her. The Japanese suffered heavy losses in this fight. In addition to the sunken "Ryujō", they lost 19 D3A1s and 6 A6M2s.

TBF-1 *Avenger* hit the target, but it was enough. "Ryujō" sank at 20:00.

After careful recognition of the American ships positions, the Japanese main forces attacked. Around 3 p.m., 27 D3A1 dive bombers and 18 A6M2 fighters from "Shōkaku" and "Zuikaku", commanded by Cdr Seki, started the attack. An hour later, the second wave of 27 D3A1s and 9 A6M2s took off, too. The B5N2 torpedo bombers remained in reserve. When the

The next clash in the Solomon Islands region began on October 26, 1942 and went down in history as the Battle of Santa Cruz Island. The day before, the advanced Japanese infantry troops, after fierce fighting, conquered the edge of Handerson airfield on Guadalcanal. The 17th Army reported a little exaggeratedly that the runways and the airfield had been taken over. It was not entirely true, but the news triggered

Torpedo drop from B5N2. The Japanese lost many aircraft of this type during the Battle of Santa Cruz Island. [Author's collection]

a chain of events. Such a signal was awaited by a large group of the Japanese Imperial Navy ships, which was supposed to block the flow of supplies for American troops on the island. Mentioned formation was divided into three parts: the team led by Rear Admiral Hiroaki Abe (two battleships, four cruisers and seven destroyers), which served as the vanguard, 1st Aircraft Carrier Squadron, commanded by Vice Admiral Nagumo ("Shōkaku", "Zuikaku", and "Zuihō"), and the Vice Admiral's Kondo support team, which included the 2nd Aircraft Carrier Squadron ("Junyo"), covered by two battleships, five cruisers and eleven destroyers. The Americans set up a strike group (USS "Hornet" and USS "Enterprise") which was commanded by a Rear Admiral Kinkaid. It was joined by the

TF-64 led by Rear Admiral Lee, which included the battleship USS "Washington", three cruisers, and five destroyers.

After receiving the news from Guadalcanal, the Japanese ships approached the island close enough that they were within the range of American reconnaissance aircraft of both the Army and the Navy. A single B-17 detected the Support Team, and not long after that the Catalina crew spotted the Vanguard Team. Eleven SBD Dauntless' took off from USS "Enterprise" with the task of accurately locating Japanese ships, but the American planes did not find their target and the battle did not take place that day. In the morning of October 26, both sides sent the recce planes. American used the forces of VS-10 and VB-10 Squadrons, while the Japanese sent 13 B5N2s

Two Nakajima B5N2s are approaching the USS "South Dakota" battleship. Battle of Santa Cruz Island. [Author's collection]

Yokosuka D4Y2 dive bomber. In 1943, these machines replaced the Aichi D3As on most Japanese aircraft carriers. [Author's collection]

The Nakajima B6N2 torpedo-bomber was a worthy successor of the B5N2 which had merited in the first phase of the war. [Author's collection]

Nakajima B5N2 from "Zuihō" aircraft carrier flying over the battleship "Yamato". Truk Atoll, March 1943. [Author's collection]

and 7 seaplanes from the Rear Admiral's Abe group. Some *Dauntless'* engaged in combat with the B5N2 they encountered, but nevertheless successfully spotted an aircraft carrier that had been identified as "Shōkaku". Two planes managed to dive and bomb the detected ship, which was actually "Zuihō". Both bombs hit the target and knocked the Japanese carrier out of action. While this attack was taking place, planes were taking off from the decks of "Shōkaku", "Zuikaku" and "Zuihō" to attack the detected Rear Admiral Kinkaid's forces. Until 7:10, 21 D3A1s, 22 B5N2s and 21 A6M2s took off, as well as one D4Y1-C *Judy* as a guide plane. The second wave

was set for the start, but the American attack delayed the take off, the planes were in the air around 8:00 a.m. Twenty D3A1s and five A6M2s took off from "Shōkaku", and 17 B5N2 and four A6M2 from Zuikaku. At 9:05 a.m., 17 D3A1s and 12 A6M2s also took off from the aircraft carrier "Junyo", which was a part of the Support Team. In total, 138 aircraft (57 D3A1s, 39 B5N2s and 42 A6M2s) set off against the Kinkaid's team. At the same time, planes also took off from the decks of the USS "Enterprise" and USS "Hornet", but there were definitely fewer of them—including the escort fighters it was only 73 machines.

Around 9:10 a.m., Japanese planes were above the target and attacked, despite strong anti-aircraft fire and numerous F4Fs in the area. The aircraft carrier USS "Hornet" was chosen as the target. The first attack was commenced by six D3A1s from "Zuikaku", followed by the B5N2 torpedo bombers. *Vals* claimed three direct hits on the ship's deck, which caused severe damage, but three of them were also struck by AA fire. Another six D3A1s dove towards the target but did not get any direct hits. Only one plane, which was hit by anti-aircraft fire, crashed against the ship's deck and superstructures, causing fur-

The B5N2 withdrawn from carriers were sent to units based in Rabaul. Lakunai airport, 194.3 [Author's collection]

B5N2 prepared for mission. At the end of 1943, most of those machines were land-based. [Author's collection]

ther damage. The B5N2 torpedo bombers from "Shōkaku", despite extremely strong barrage of fire and *Wildcat* attacks, managed to hit with two torpedoes—the first in the midship and the second in the stern of the ship. USS "Hornet's" damage was already very serious, and she fought to survive, but the Japanese losses were also extremely tough. Ten B5N2s, 11 D3A1s and 3 A6M2s were shot down, and 14 more planes suffered such a heavy damage that they did not reach their mother carriers. In total Japanese lost 38 aircraft during the first wave of attack.

Soon the American group was approached by the second wave of the Japanese attack, which was delayed. They aimed for the previously unattacked USS "Enterprise", which now was a target for the D3A1 dive bombers, but the murderous AA artillery fire from the aircraft carrier and other ships weakened the momentum and made it difficult for the Japanese to attack. Only two bombs hit the ship directly, and the damage caused by their explosions was not that serious.

At the same time, another group of B5N2 torpedo bombers, most likely from the "Zuikaku", was approaching the slowly sinking and covered with smoke USS "Hornet". Seeing this, the commander of the formation, Capt. Imajuki decided to attack the second carrier— USS "Enterprise". Unfortunately, none of the torpedoes hit the hard manoeuvring ship, and the Japanese suffered serious losses. It was not the end of the battle, as planes that took off from the carrier "Junyo" appeared on the battlefield. Some of them attacked the USS "Enterprise," but did not cause any serious damage. Others, failing to find the carrier, attacked the remaining American ships, including the battleship USS "South Dakota" and the cruiser USS "San Juan". Both of these units were hit by single bombs, but they did not cause any serious damage.

In the afternoon of the same day, the Japanese air force attacked again. Fourteen B5N2s armed with 800 kg armour-piercing bombs, two D3A1s and thirteen A6M2s fighters took off from the "Zuikaku" and "Junyo"

By the end of 1943, the B5N2 was already obsolete and it was transferred from aircraft carriers to land bases. [Author's collection]

B5N2 armed with the torpedo. In the second half of the war, these meritorious machines were moved to the secondary tasks. [Author's collection]

aircraft carriers. Their task was to finish off the damaged USS "Hornet", which was still floating on the water. The formation arrived at the target around 15:40. Only one bomb hit directly, but that was enough. USS "Hornet's" commander, Cdr. Manson, ordered to abandon the ship. The burning wreck did not sink until late at night. The battle was over, but the losses suffered by the Japanese were very severe. Two aircraft carriers ("Shōkaku" and "Zuihō") were damaged, and 95 aircraft and crews were lost.

The Battle of Santa Cruz Island was the last major clash in which the D3A1s and B5N2s bombers played the role of basic attack aircraft. Soon, a newer version of the D3A2 Model 22 was introduced to Japanese aircraft carriers, but by the beginning of 1943 it was also obsolete. Most of the D3As were used in land-based units (only a small number of these machines remained on board of light aircraft carriers) and were replaced by the Aichi D4Y *Judy*. The situation was similar in the case of the B5N2, extremely meritorious for the Imperial Navy in the first phase of the war. A worthy successor was the Nakajima B6N *Tenzan*. A small number of

*Kates* remained on light aircraft carriers due to the shorter run-up distance than in the case of the B6N. Rest of the B5N2s, same as D3As, ended up in land-based units. However, it was not the end of combat operations for both types.

At the beginning of February 1943, the evacuation of Japanese troops from Guadalcanal began, and the deck planes from the 1st Aircraft Carrier Squadron, based on land, were used to cover the retreating troops. The evacuation ended on February 8, but the Japanese had no intention of leaving the US forces grouped in Guadalcanal alone.

On April 1, 1943, Operation I-Go began—an offensive against the Allied forces in Solomon Islands and New Guinea. The planes from the 21st and 26th Koku Sentai based in Rabaul, reinforced by machines delegated from the 1st and 2nd Aircraft Carrier Squadrons, including 65 D3A2s and 5 B5N2s, were assigned to execute the air part of the plan. Planes attacked with varying luck. Among other targets they bombed an airport on Russel Island and the Tulagi anchorage. The last operation of Operation I-Go took place on April 14, when 44 D3A2s and 75 G4M1s, escorted 129 A6M2s, attacked targets

in Milne Bay, succeeding only with sinking one ship.

The end of Operation I-Go did not mean that the Japanese air force was no longer carrying out attacks in the area. On June 30, 1943, planes from Rabaul made several raids on American landings in New Georgia and Rendova. On August 15, the Japanese reacted immediately to the landing of US marines on the island of Vella Lavella, sending almost all of the 21st Koku Sentai against the landing troops. Already at 8:00, the Americans were attacked by a dozen or so of D3A2s, but the assault did not bring the expected results. Then the B5N2 attacked, followed by another wave of D3A2s and A6M3s fighters. The Japanese operated with great determination, but did not manage to eliminate the bridgehead, and the unloading of soldiers and equipment continued uninterrupted. *Wildcats* and *Corsairs*, as well as anti-aircraft artillery, took a bloody toll—eight D3A2s, two B5N2s and no less than seven A6M3s were shot down. In addition, eight A6M2s and two D3A2s were destroyed during an evening raid by US Navy planes at Bunin airport, where some of the Japanese machines were based.

The B5N2s and D3A2s withdrawn from the aircraft carriers have joined the units stationed at Rabaul, a Japanese base in New Britain. Between September 28 and October 1, 1943, 157 aircraft from the 1st Aircraft Squadron were transferred there, which was a significant strengthening of the forces. Among them were 40 B5N2s and 45 D3A2s. This happened

for a reason, as the Japanese Imperial Navy headquarters were preparing another operation in the area, codenamed Ro-Go. It was supposed to be a more effective I-Go replay. It began on October 15, 1943. Fifteen D3A2s escorted by 39 A6M2s raided on Allied ships in the Gulf of Oro. The action ended in a complete failure, because the Japanese formation was intercepted by around 70 American F4Fs and P-38s and literally was shot from the air—only one D3A2 survived! On October 17, another action of this type was carried out against Finschhafen. This time the Japanese losses were not that big, but the attack's result was negligible.

Another target was the American landing on the west coast of Bougainville, launched on November 1, 1943. A hastily assembled Japanese formation consisting of 16 D3A2s, 9 G4Ms and 79 *Reisen* fighters set out to destroy the invasion forces. The cost of that operation was high, although did not cause much damage to the enemy. Eight bombers and 28 fighters did not return to Rabaul.

The Allies were closer to the Japanese base, and Rabaul was exposed to incessant air raids by heavy B-24 *Liberator* bombers and deck planes taking off from USS "Saratoga" and USS "Princeton" carriers. On November 5, 1943, the Americans launched massive air raids on this base. The deck planes from the above-mentioned carriers were the first to hit, and the next day the destruction was finished by 5th Air Force bombers based on land. Already in the evening of November 5, the Japanese tried

to neutralize the aircraft carriers by sending 18 B5N2s armed with torpedoes in their direction, but the attack was unsuccessful. The Japanese pilots did report the sinking of the USS "Saratoga" and damage to the USS "Princeton" upon their return, but in fact none of the dropped torpedoes hit the target.

The Americans were not satisfied with the results of the attack on Rabaul and repeated it a few days later. This time, planes from five air-

**B5N2 "Yellow KEB-306" captured by the Americans. [Author's collection]**

**H-6 radar antenna mounted on the leading edge of the left wing of the B5N2 (KEB-306). Plane was captured by the Americans at Saipan. [Author's collection]**

Unfolding the B5N2 wings (KEB-306). The machine was brought to a flying state and thoroughly tested. [Author's collection]

Nakajima B5N2 (KEB-306) among the ruined buildings at Saipan. 1944 [Author's collection]

craft carriers: USS "Saratoga", USS "Princeton", USS "Bunker Hill", USS "Essex" and USS "Independence" took part in the attack. The Japanese reacted quickly, and after the first raids they sent 27 D3A2 and D4Y1 dive bombers, 14 B5N2 torpedo bombers and a dozen G4Ms against the American group. The entire formation was covered by about 70 A6M *Zero* fighters. All aircraft came from the 1st Aircraft Carrier Squadron and the 25th Koku Sentai. The attack was unsuccessful, though, because the Japanese were intercepted on the way to their destination. Only few planes managed to hit the ships. The losses were very high—all of the B5N2s, 17 D3A2s, two D4Y1s and a few G4Ms were shot down. Within a month, Japanese aviation in Rabaul lost almost 70% of its aircraft.

On February 17, 1944, seven of the "Shōkaku's" B5N2 torpedo squadrons based on Truk, carried out one of the last operations in which aircraft of this type played the assault role. In the darkness, flying just above the water surface, thanks to which they were not detected by radars, bombers crept near the American aircraft carriers that were conducting operations against the island. One of the dropped torpedoes hit the USS "Interpid". It did not cause too much damage, but the ship was taken out of action. The biggest achievement of the Japanese in this action was the fact that, despite the huge advantage of the opponent, all B5N2s returned to the base.

## Swan song

The last great battle of aircraft carriers during World War II was the Operation A-Go (Battle of the Philippine Sea) on June 19–20, 1944. According to Japanese plans, the battle was to be fought in the southern Philippine Sea, in the Paau-Mariana Islands region, which would allow for the support of about 350 land-based aircraft.

The reorganized and rebuilt fleet of Japanese carriers—Kido Kantai—set off towards the Marians on June 15. It consisted of nine aircraft carriers grouped in three squadrons: 1st Squadron ("Taihō", "Shōkaku", "Zuikaku"), 2nd Squadron ("Junyo", "Hiyō", "Ryuhō") and 3rd Squadron ("Chitose", "Chiyoda", "Zuihō"). A total of 439 aircraft were based on their decks. Most of them were new-type machines. Only 36 D3A2 dive bombers of 652nd Kokutai were used on "Junyo" and "Hiyō".

Operation A-Go ended in a complete defeat of the Japanese. Three aircraft carriers (including the newest "Taihō") sank, and deck aviation was practically wiped out. The obsolete D3A2s played no role in the battle anymore and were decimated by the F6F *Hellcat* fighters and an-

ti-aircraft fire from the USS "Wasp" and USS "Bunker Hill" aircraft carriers that they tried to attack. The result of the battle was largely influenced by the poor training of Japanese pilots—a problem that became increasingly acute in the second half of the war.

B5N2 *Kate's* swan song was an attempt made by 20 of these machines to attack one of the American escort carriers on June 24, 1944. All the planes were shot down by the F6F air patrol on their way to target. After this action, they were withdrawn from the front line and assigned to patrol tasks and aviation schools. Some of these worn-out machines took part in the fight once more, for the last time. During the battles for Okinawa in March and April 1945, they were used by Kamikaze pilots.

Little known and rarely mentioned in the literature is the participation of B5N2 in the fighting with the USSR in August 1945. The area between Hokkaido and Aleutians was patrolled by 553rd Kokutai stationed in this area, which was equipped with 13 Nakajima B6N *Tenzans* and 21 old B5N2 *Kates*. In addition, several Hokuto Kokutai B5N2s were based on the Kurils. On August 10, 1945, machines from the latter unit attacked targets in Kamchatka. Although a ceasefire was in force from August 15, combat operations in the Kuril area continued, as Soviet units of the Pacific Fleet landed on more islands of this archipelago, seeking to occupy the largest possible territory.

Most likely, the last action of B5N2 during the World War II was the attack on a Soviet convoy and sinking a minesweeper by four B5N2s from Hokuto Kokutai. It took place on August 18, 1945.

**B5N2 of Yokosuka Kokutai, 1944. In the second half of 1944, B5N2s were withdrawn from the frontline and mainly used for patrol duties. [Author's collection]**

**B5N2 photographed at the airport in Jacquinot Bay in the south-eastern part of New Britain. [Author's collection]**

Tests of the B5N2 captured at Saipan (KEB-306) and restored by the Americans to the flight state. [Author's collection]

The B5N2 (KEB-306), captured at Saipan, reached the United States on July 28, 1944. It was transported on board of the USS "Copahee" escort carrier. [Public domain]

B5N2 T.A.I.C. 6 (ex-KEB-306) takes off during the tests conducted in the States. [Author's collection]

## Bibliography

T. Nozawa, T. Iwata *Encyclopedia of Japanese Aircraft 1900–1945*, Vol. 5, *Nakajima Aircraft*, Suppon-Kyodo, 1983.

D. Thorpe, E. Maloney, *Tora! Tora! Tora! Pearl Harbor*, 1999.

T. Prusinowska, M. Skwiot, *Pearl Harbor 1941*, 1995.

T. Januszewski, K. Zalewski, *Japońskie samoloty marynarki vol. 1, vol. 2*, Lampart 2000.

S. Fleischer, Z. Szeremeta, *Aichi D3A Val, Nakajima B5N Kate*, Militaria 2001.

Война в воздухе 025, *D3A Val, B5N Kate – ударные самолёты японского флота*.

Maru Mechanic.

Koku-Fan.

MONOGRAFIE MONOGRAPHS

# Nakajima B5N Kate

Drawings/Rysunki: Anirudh Rao

B5N1 "KATE"

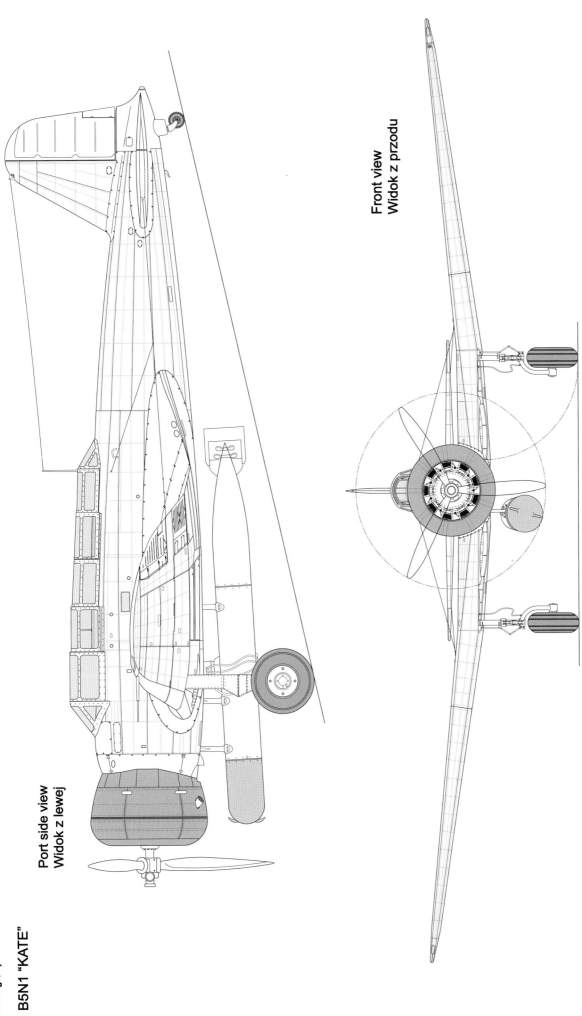

Port side view
Widok z lewej

Front view
Widok z przodu

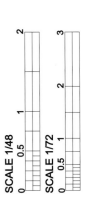

SCALE 1/48
0    0.5    1    2

SCALE 1/72
0    0.5    1    2    3

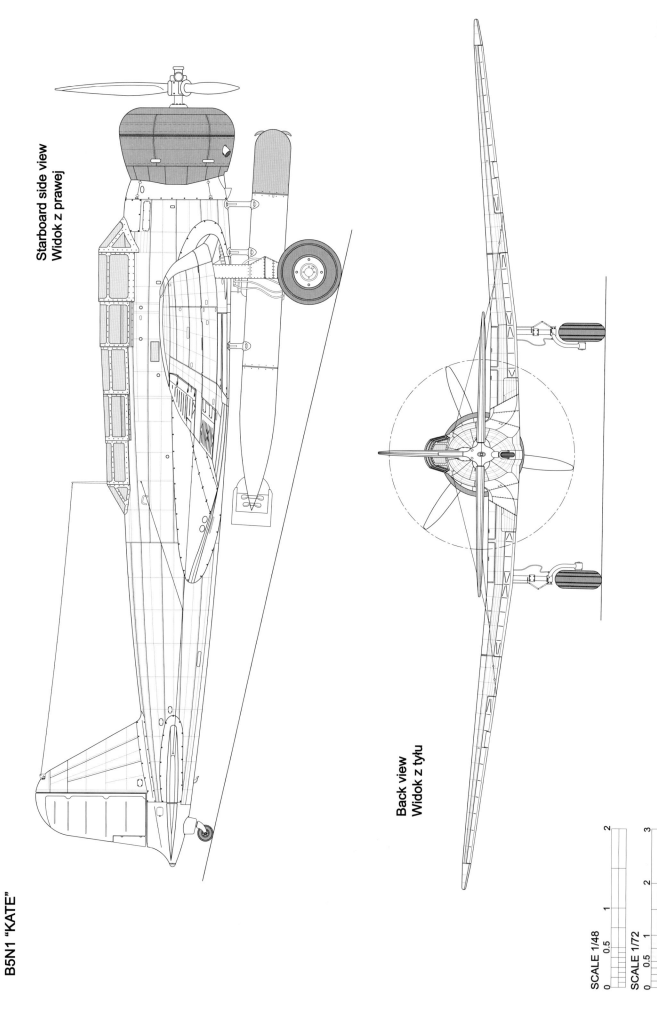

# Nakajima B5N Kate
**Drawings/Rysunki: Anirudh Rao**

B5N1 "KATE"

Starboard side view
Widok z prawej

Back view
Widok z tytu

SCALE 1/48

SCALE 1/72

**Nakajima B5N Kate**
**Drawings/Rysunki: Anirudh Rao**

B5N1 "KATE"

Top view
Widok z góry

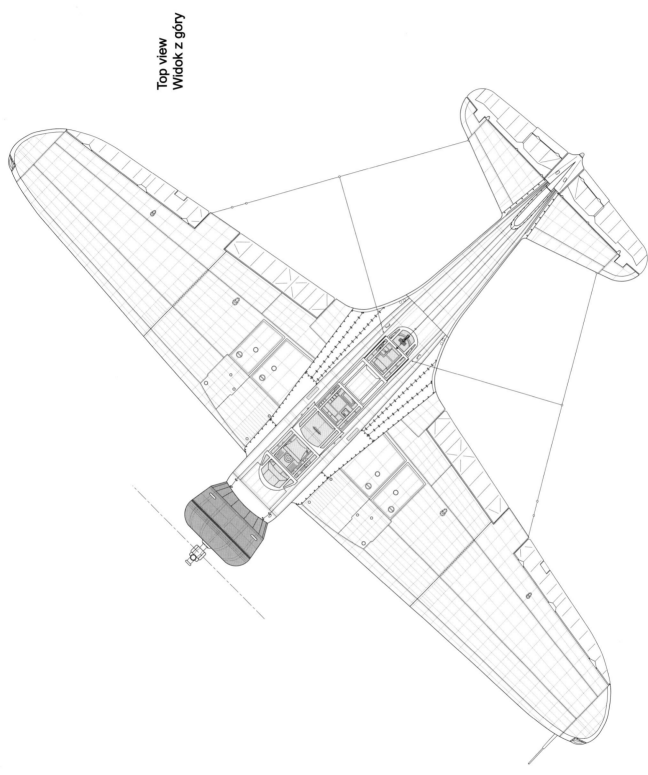

SCALE 1/72

**Nakajima B5N Kate**
Drawings/Rysunki: Anirudh Rao

B5N1 "KATE"

Bottom view
Widok z dołu

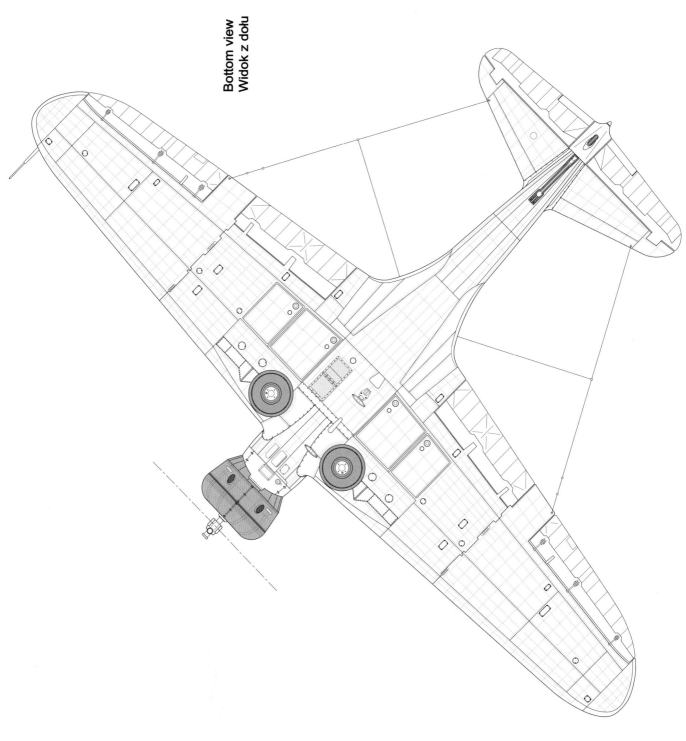

SCALE 1/72

0    0.5    1    2    3

B5N1 "KATE"

F - F'

E - E'

D - D'

C - C'

B - B'

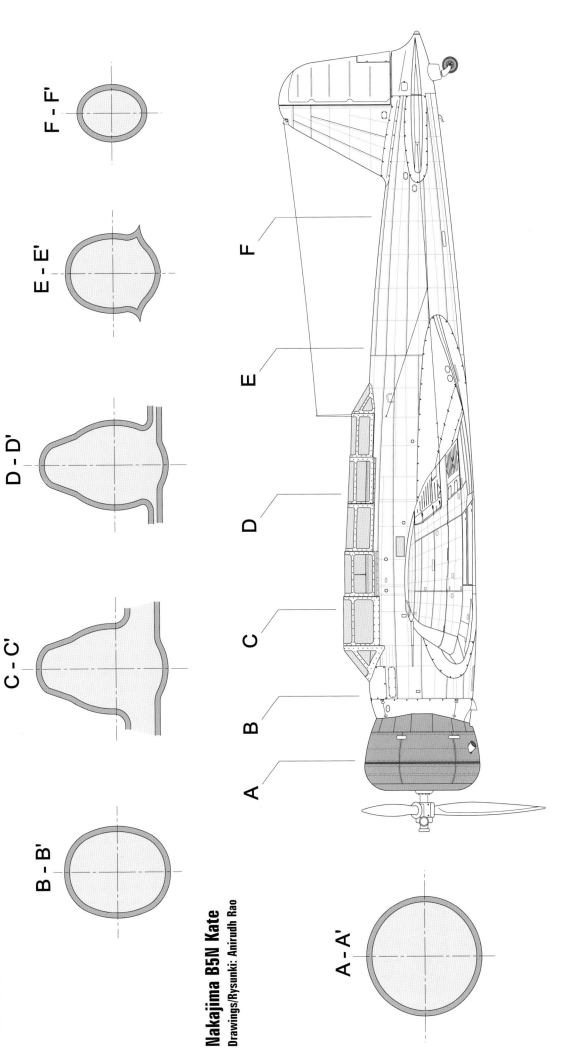

F

E

D

C

B

A

A - A'

**Nakajima B5N Kate**
Drawings/Rysunki: Anirudh Rao

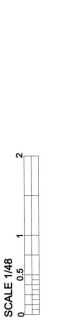

SCALE 1/48

0    0.5    1    2

KAGERO

B5N1 "KATE"

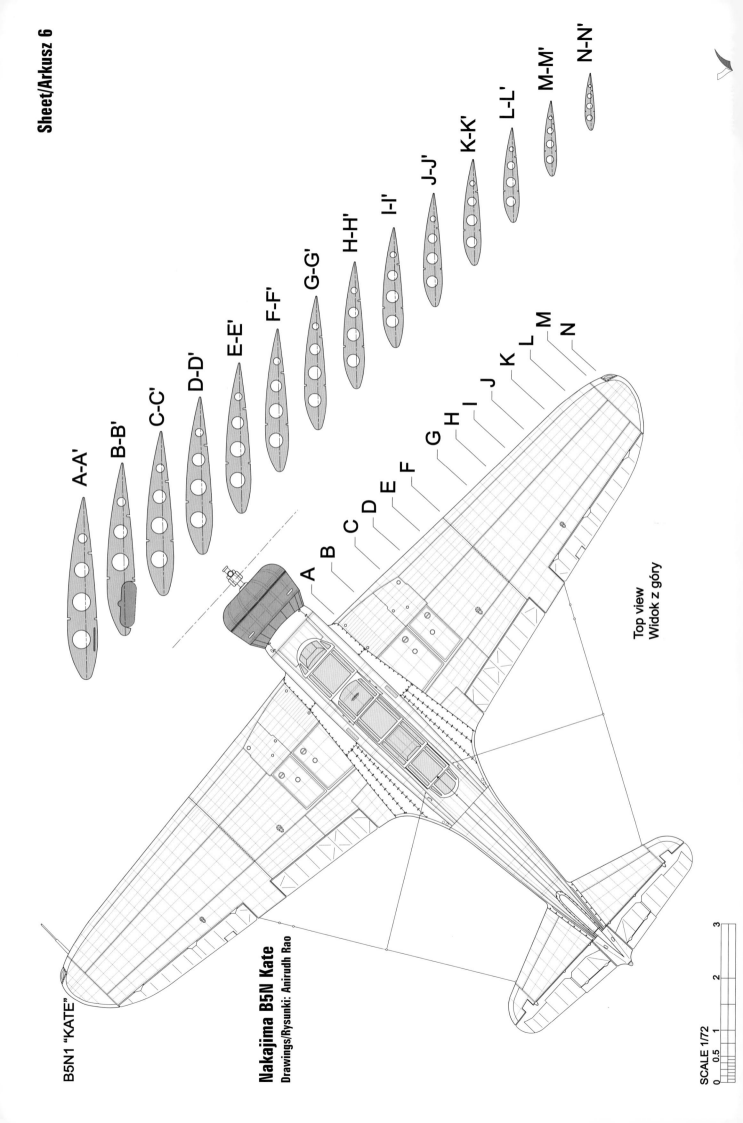

A-A'
B-B'
C-C'
D-D'
E-E'
F-F'
G-G'
H-H'
I-I'
J-J'
K-K'
L-L'
M-M'
N-N'

A
B
C
D
E
F
G
H
I
J
K
L
M
N

**Nakajima B5N Kate**
Drawings/Rysunki: Anirudh Rao

Top view
Widok z góry

SCALE 1/72
0  0.5  1  2  3

**Nakajima B5N Kate**

Drawings/Rysunki: Anirudh Rao

B5N1 "KATE"

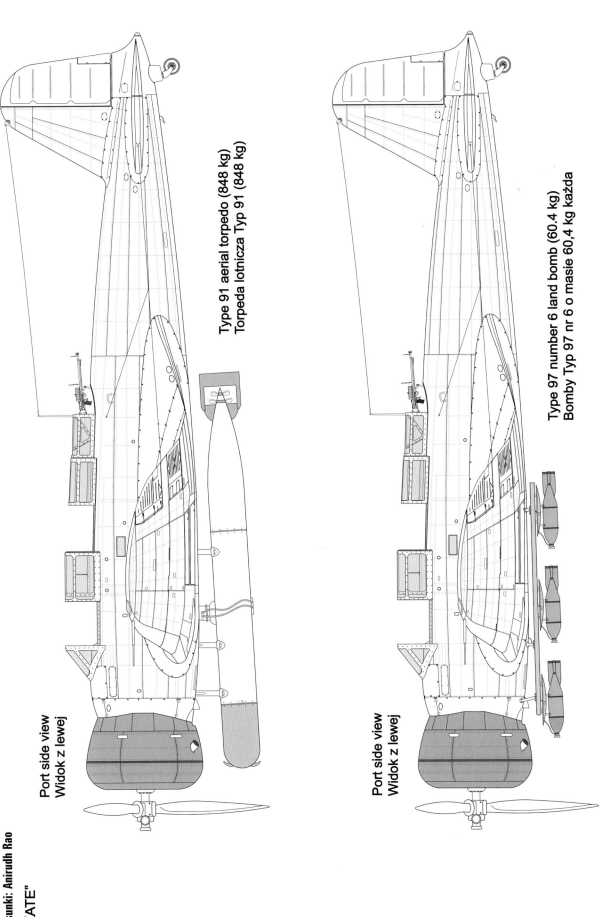

Type 91 aerial torpedo (848 kg)
Torpeda lotnicza Typ 91 (848 kg)

Port side view
Widok z lewej

Type 97 number 6 land bomb (60.4 kg)
Bomby Typ 97 nr 6 o masie 60,4 kg każda

Port side view
Widok z lewej

SCALE 1/48

| 0 | 0.5 | 1 | | 2 |

**Nakajima B5N Kate**
Drawings/Rysunki: Anirudh Rao

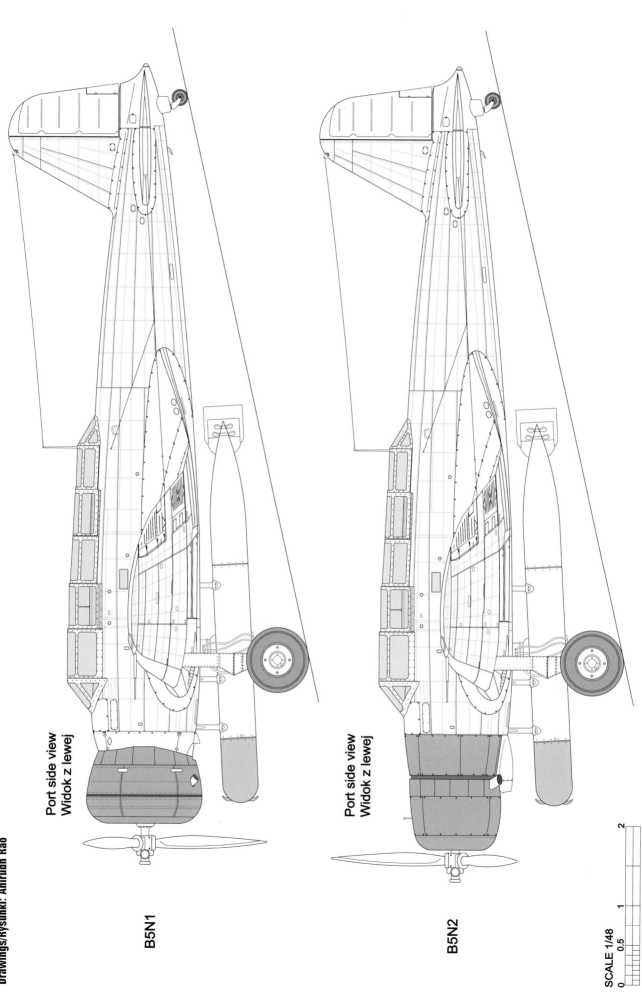

Port side view
Widok z lewej

B5N1

Port side view
Widok z lewej

B5N2

SCALE 1/48

0    0.5    1    2

# Nakajima B5N Kate
**Drawings/Rysunki: Anirudh Rao**

B5N2 "KATE"

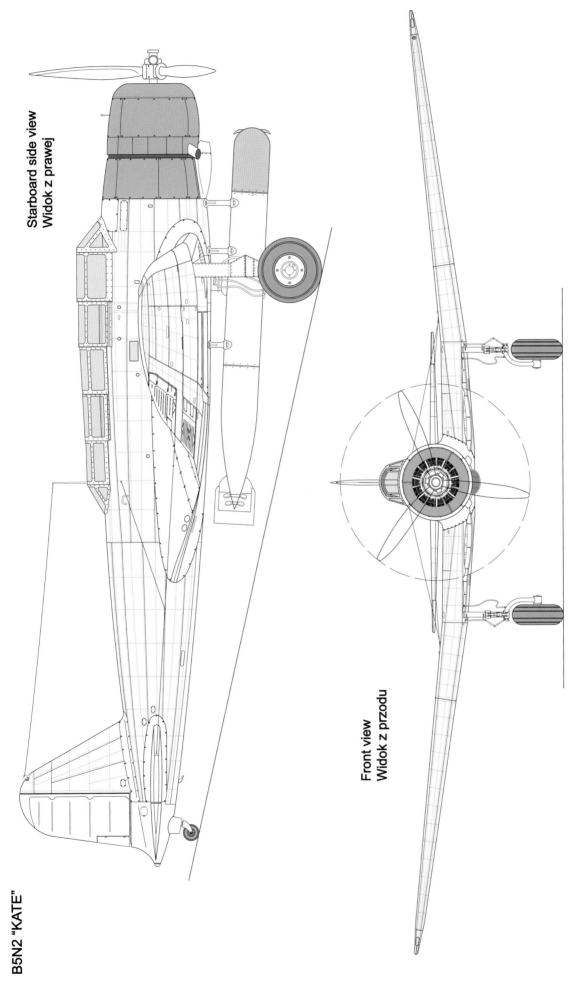

Starboard side view
Widok z prawej

Front view
Widok z przodu

SCALE 1/48
0      0.5      1      2

SCALE 1/72
0      0.5      1      2      3

Top view
Widok z góry

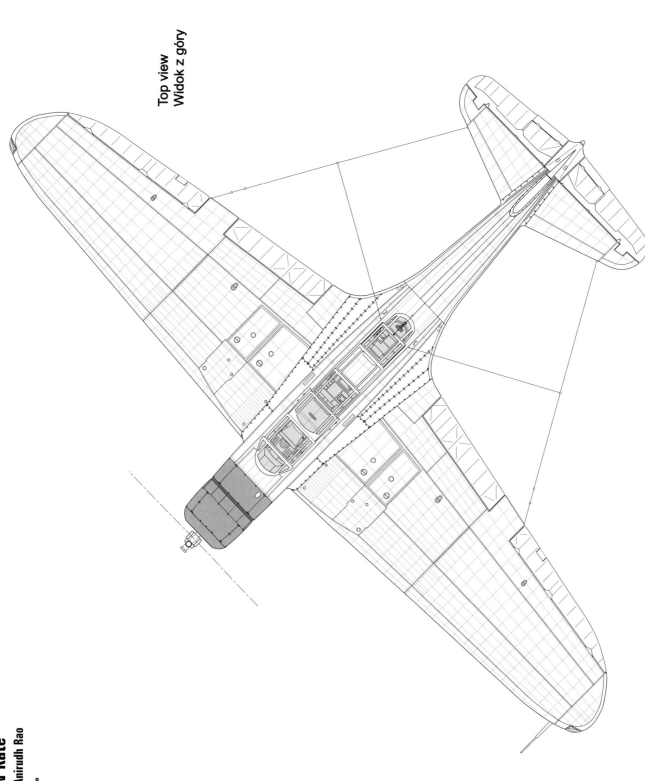

SCALE 1/72

0   0.5   1   2   3

**Nakajima B5N Kate**
Drawings/Rysunki: Anirudh Rao

B5N2 "KATE"

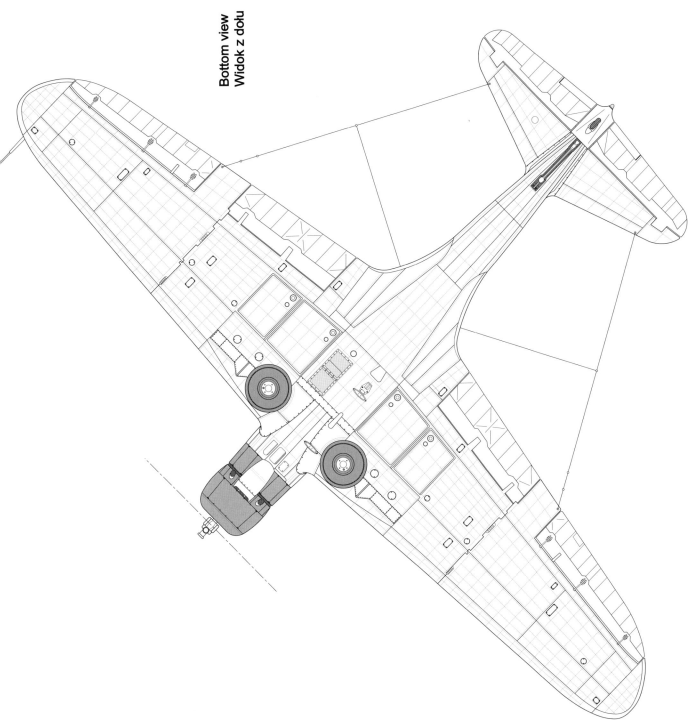

Bottom view
Widok z dołu

0  0.5  1        2        3

# Nakajima B5N Kate
**Drawings/Rysunki: Anirudh Rao**

B5N2 "KATE"

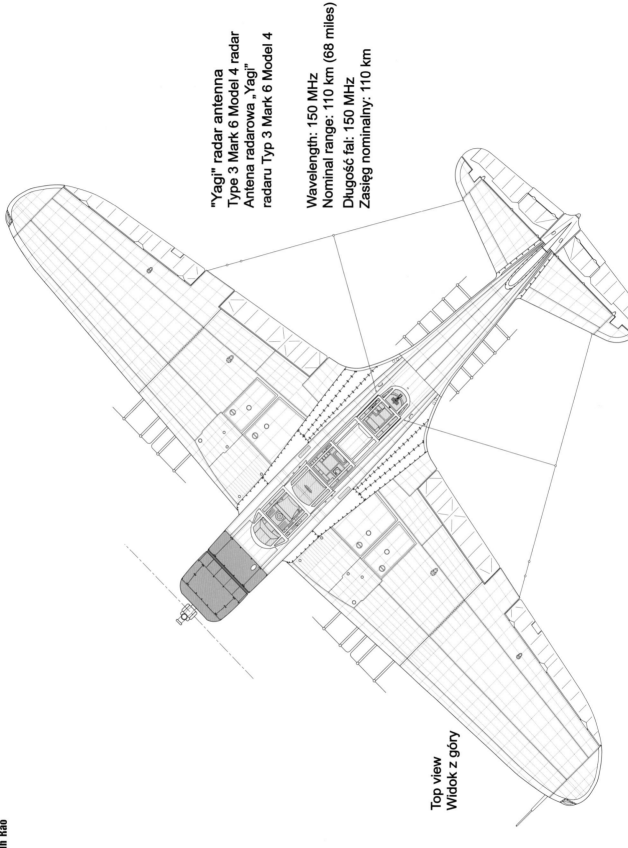

"Yagi" radar antenna
Type 3 Mark 6 Model 4 radar
Antena radarowa „Yagi"
radaru Typ 3 Mark 6 Model 4

Wavelength: 150 MHz
Nominal range: 110 km (68 miles)
Długość fal: 150 MHz
Zasięg nominalny: 110 km

Top view
Widok z góry

SCALE 1/72

0   0.5   1        2        3

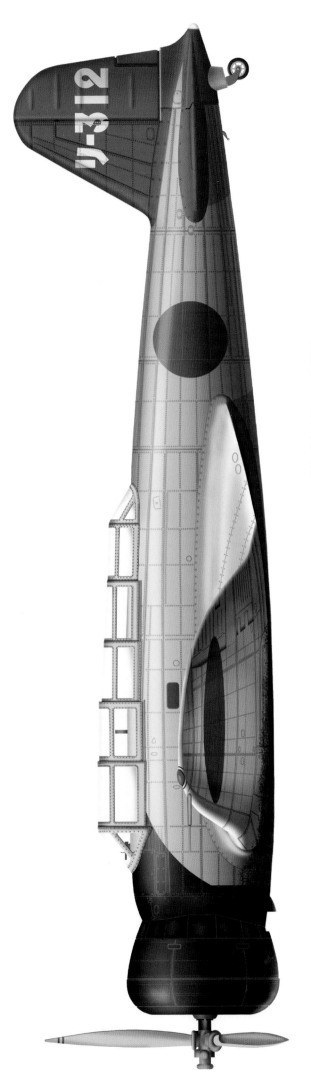

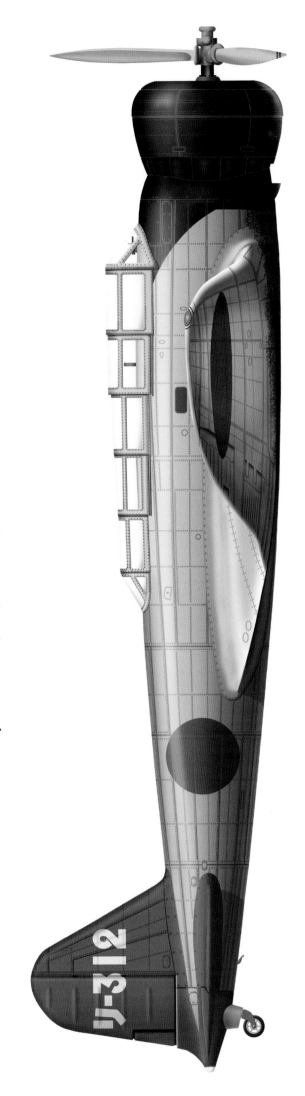

**Nakajima B5N1 Model 11 (Ru-312) from the training Hyakrihara Kokutai. Hyakrihara, early 1939**

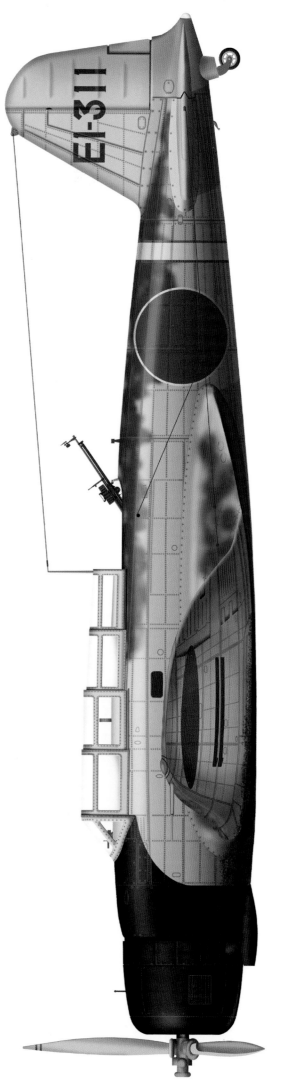

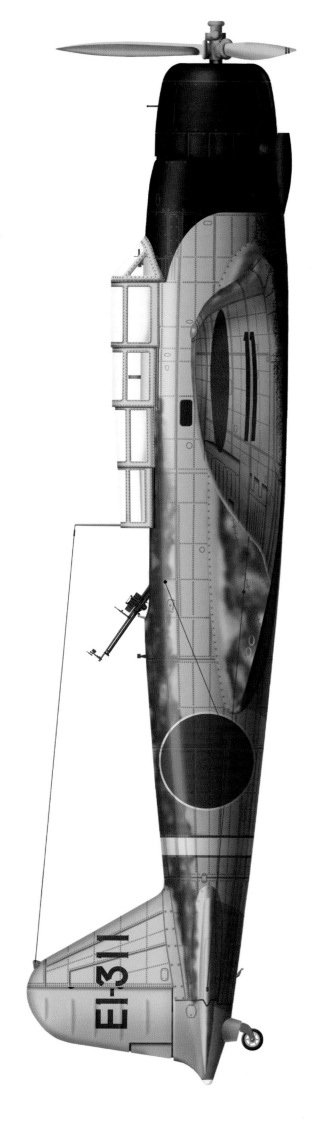

Nakajima B5N2 (EI-311) from the "Shōkaku" aircraft carrier. The upper surfaces were painted green shortly before the attack on Pearl Harbor. It was done in a rush and not very accurately.

*Painted by Alexey Valyaev-Zaitsev*

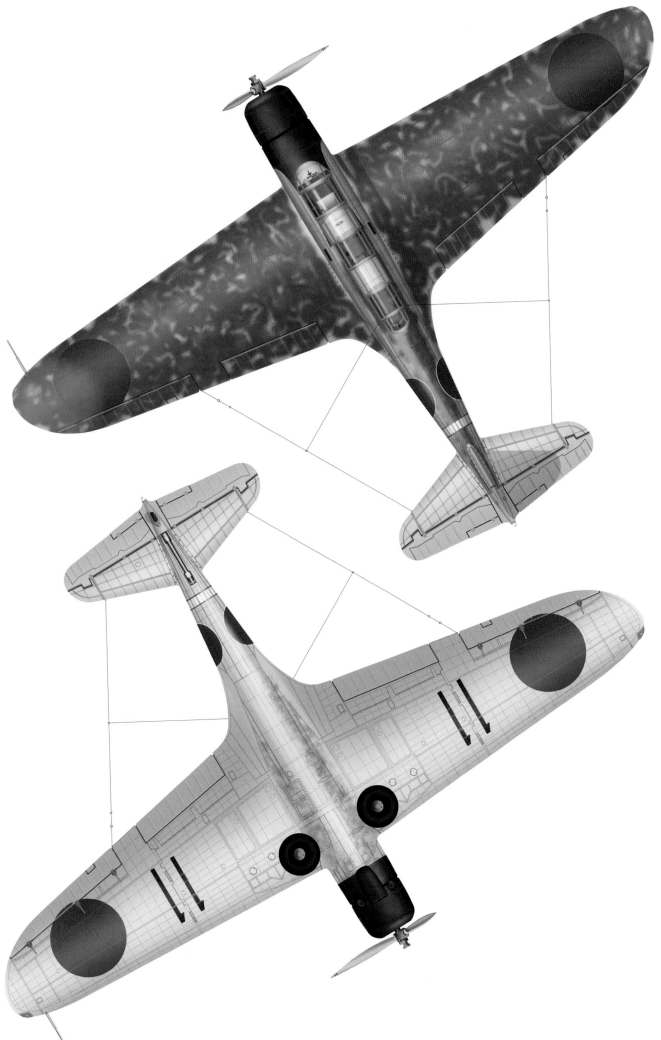

*Painted by Alexey Valyaev-Zaitsev*

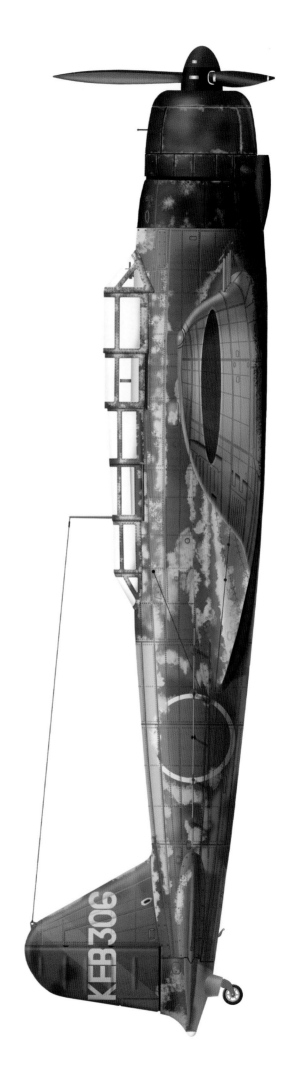

Nakajima B5N2 Kate of the 931st Kokutai, equipped with H-6 radar. The machine was used for patrolling and search for enemy submarines. In June 1944, after the capture of Saipan, the Americans found this plane at Asilto airport and after some time transported it to the USA, where it was thoroughly tested.

Painted by Alexey Valyaev-Zaitsev

**Light machine gun Type 92 with a 97-round drum magazine.**

*Painted by Alexey Valyaev-Zaitsev*

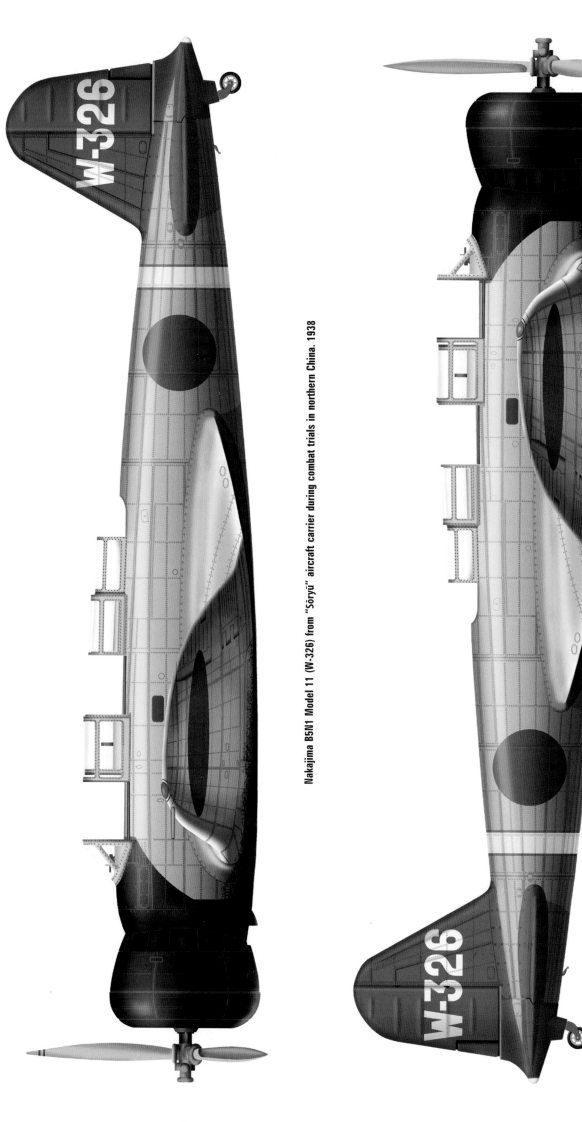

**Nakajima B5N1 Model 11 (W-326) from "Sōryū" aircraft carrier during combat trials in northern China. 1938**

*Painted by Alexey Valyaev-Zaitsev*

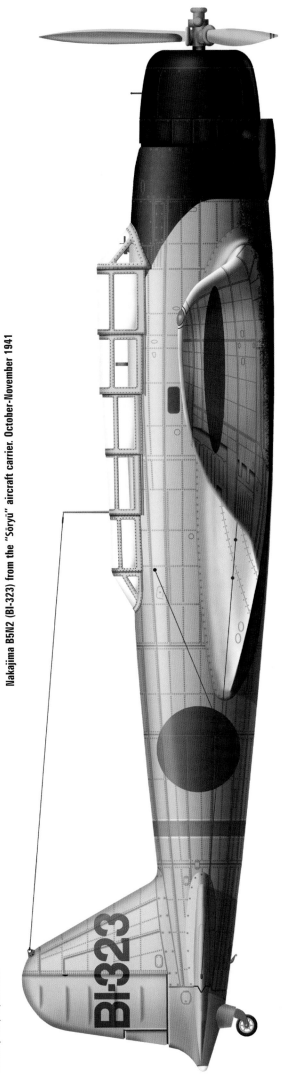

*Painted by Alexey Valyaev-Zaitsev*

**Nakajima B5N2 (BI-323) from the "Sōryū" aircraft carrier. October-November 1941**

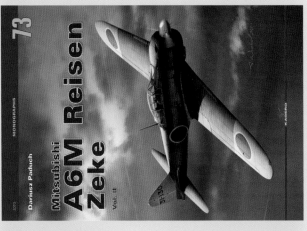
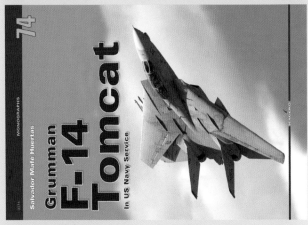

# WE RECOMMEND

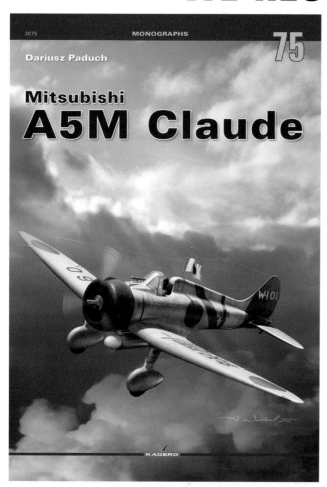

MONOGRAPHS 75

3075

Dariusz Paduch

Mitsubishi
**A5M Claude**

KAGERO

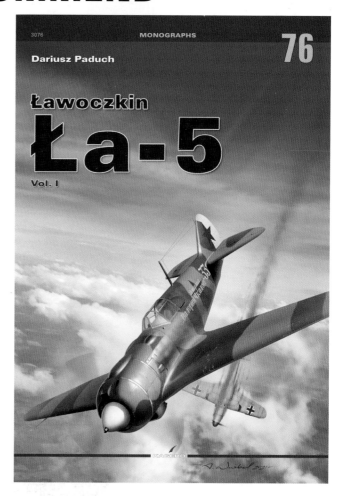

MONOGRAPHS 76

3076

Dariusz Paduch

Ławoczkin
**Ła-5**

Vol. I

KAGERO

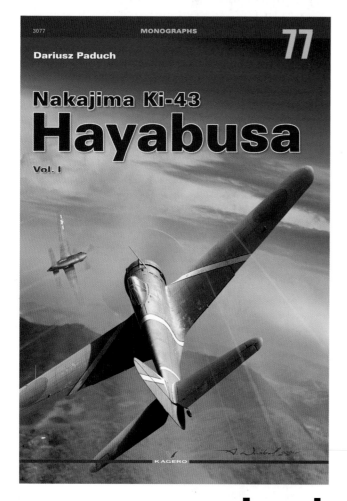

MONOGRAPHS 77

3077

Dariusz Paduch

Nakajima Ki-43
**Hayabusa**

Vol. I

KAGERO

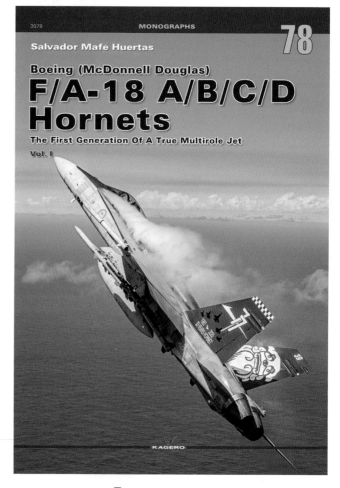

MONOGRAPHS 78

3078

Salvador Mafé Huertas

Boeing (McDonnell Douglas)
**F/A-18 A/B/C/D Hornets**
The First Generation Of A True Multirole Jet

Vol. I

KAGERO

## shop.kagero.pl